Therapeutic Justice and Addicted Parents

A Family Treatment Court Evaluation

Heidee McMillin

LFB Scholarly Publishing LLC
El Paso 2012

Library of Congress Cataloging-in-Publication Data

McMillin, Heidee Eileen, 1964-
Therapeutic justice and addicted parents : a family treatment court evaluation / Heidee McMillin.
p. cm. -- (Criminal justice: recent scholarship)
Includes bibliographical references and index.
ISBN 978-1-59332-514-5 (hardcover : alk. paper)
1. Domestic relations courts--United States. 2. Drug courts--United States. 3. Drug abuse--Treatment--Law and legislation--United States. 4.
Drug abuse--United States--Prevention. 5. Drug addicts--Rehabilitation--United States. I. Title.
KF505.5.M36 2012
345.73'02770269--dc23
2012001980

ISBN 978-1-59332-514-5

Printed on acid-free 250-year-life paper.

Manufactured in the United States of America.

Table of Contents

List of Tables and Figures

Acknowledgements

With deepest gratitude to Nicholas Lovrich, David Brody, Michael J. Erp, and Merry Armstrong.

Introduction

This research provides a rare, in-depth examination of a family drug treatment court. The researcher monitored clients of a family drug treatment court via courtroom observations, treatment records review, post-program client interviews and surveys, to document the program's effect with respect to client sobriety, housing and income stability, and family reunification. Study subjects for this evaluation included the first group of program graduates who matriculated in October 2003, through clients who entered the program by December 31, 2005. The researcher also recorded observations in weekly drug court treatment team meetings from 2003 through 2005, and interviewed team members to examine the administrative processes of a family drug treatment court.

Early outcome measures for drug courts were traditionally two-fold, including only recidivism and relapse. The National Treatment Improvement Evaluation Study 1991-1996 was one of the first to examine more diverse outcome measures, such as changes in employment rates and public assistance use for drug court clients both one year before and one year after treatment (note this was for drug court clients, not family treatment court clients). Post-treatment findings included a 19% increase in employment rates, an 11% decrease in public assistance, and a 43% decrease in homelessness. These expanded outcome measures, along with family reunification have become useful in evaluating family drug treatment courts.

Although the issue that brings clients to either adult drug court or family treatment court is substantially the same – namely, substance abuse, the clients, consequences, and appropriate definition of success are arguably very different for these two groups. Drug court clients are predominately male, while family treatment court clients are overwhelmingly female (Roman, Townsend & Bhadi, 2003; Office of Justice Programs, 2000; Family Drug Court Activity Update, 2000). Drug court clients have all been charged with a drug crime, while family treatment court clients have had their children removed from their home due to their drug use; they commonly have no pending criminal charges and may have no criminal history. While remaining drug- and recidivism-free for drug offenders is a proper and admirable goal, in family treatment court much more than personal rectitude is at stake. People can lose their parental status - their family *identity* - if they cannot stay clean. For drug courts, the issue is primarily criminal; for family treatment courts, the issue is primarily relational. Because of these clear differences, and due to the scarcity of published work on family drug treatment court evaluations, this research focused on findings derived from a process and outcome evaluation of a family treatment court (FTC) in the Pacific Northwest.

The research data collected for the FTC analysis consisted of the following five elements:

- 200 hours of recorded courtroom observations
- 200 hours of recorded treatment court team meeting observations
- Review of treatment intake assessments, client treatment progress reports, and portions of clients' State Department of Social and Health Services (DSHS) files
- Post-program interviews and survey data collected from FTC clients
- Interviews of treatment court team members.

The triangulation of data sources enhanced data integrity and provided an accurate picture of the outcomes experienced by both clients and the control group associated with the FTC.

Individuals in this study were examined through the theoretical lens of Sampson and Laub's *Life Course Theory* of deviant behavior (1993:8). The theory in question posits that life pathways or *trajectories*, representing long-term patterns of behavior, are marked by a sequence of *transitions* or life events that can result in permanent change in the direction of a life trajectory. The interlocking nature of *trajectories* and *transitions* may generate *turning points*, or a noteworthy change in the life course. The same event or transition followed by different adaptations can lead to different trajectories (Elder, 1985: 31-32 & 35). For example, in this analysis, the parents' life trajectories are on a path of recurrent drug use that has brought them to a potential transition where the state has removed their children from their care. This study was based on the hypothesis that participation in the year-long, intensive outpatient FTC program will serve as a turning point that changes clients' life trajectory for the better. The expectations are that treatment group clients, as compared to the "early out" group and the "comparison" group will:

- Be more likely to have their dependency dismissed
- Have less subsequent Child Protective Service (CPS) involvement
- Remain clean and sober for longer periods
- Be more likely to secure gainful employment
- Be more likely to establish permanent housing
- Be more likely to attend and complete school or skills training

The family drug court program can be judged effective to the extent it assists clients to achieve the above-stated program objectives.

The process evaluation of the FTC program includes two years (January 2004 through December 2005). The process evaluation examines the FTC treatment team's group dynamics, and documents the extent to which clients were treated equitably by the treatment team regarding compliance with program requirements, receipt of incentives, and the imposition of sanctions.

This research identifies the strengths of this program, the areas where it falls short of ideal expectations, and discusses the ability of the family drug court to serve its intended target population. This research also contributes to the limited body of literature concerning family treatment court research. This research begins with a discussion of the evolution of the drug court movement in the United States.

CHAPTER 1

The Drug Court Movement

The first drug court program became operational in 1989 in Dade County, Florida. This problem-solving court came into being as a practical response to the extreme pressure the courts and correctional system experienced as a result of the explosion of drug cases that accompanied the Reagan Administration's War on Drugs. While the primary reason behind the innovation was to promote court efficiency rather than to improve the life prospects of addicts, the court chose to address the problem of the excessive number of non-violent drug offenders through rehabilitation of their drug-addiction (Gallas, 2004).

Under traditional practices, there was little judicial input into the content of treatment programs for drug-involved defendants, and little two-way communication occurred between the court and the treatment provider. Other than when the provider was required to notify the court of an individual's completion of treatment or failure to comply with the requirements of the treatment process, the communication between judge and treatment professionals was virtually nonexistent. Judges fully delegated the responsibility for appropriate treatment and offender supervision to probation officers and treatment providers.

In the "refer-out" model, treatment providers controlled admission screening (some resisted accepting criminal justice clients), the level of care to be provided (the mix and location of services, from outpatient to inpatient – including ancillary services), and the termination process Typically, treatment providers could discharge an "uncooperative" client that was having a difficult time fulfilling the conditions of the program. What were seen by treatment professionals as appropriate elements of a sound treatment process were often seen as self-interested, self-serving, and inappropriately selective procedures by criminal justice professionals. Such critics of the treatment model saw these programs as willing to take only the most treatable among the criminal justice candidates ("skimming"), and overly likely to reject or quickly terminate the more difficult clients (those most in need of treatment) presented by the criminal justice system (Goldkamp, 2000).

The drug court innovation sought to build a new approach to the problem based on four concepts:

- A "hands-on" judiciary engaged in pro-active problem-solving
- A strong supervisory and case management approach
- Accessible and relevant treatment services
- A closer relationship between treatment providers and the legal actors involved in a court-treatment process in which the judge controlled program admission and termination (Goldkamp, 2000).

Thus, the drug court treatment provider could not unilaterally reject difficult criminal justice clients accepted into the drug court and could not, without judicial approval, terminate participants when they had failed to comply with treatment program requirements (Goldkamp, 2000).

Drug courts broadened the aims of the justice system beyond the necessary basic concerns for public safety to include health, substance abuse prevention and treatment, lifestyle improvement, employment, housing, parenting, and other core welfare objectives designed to improve the lives of participants and to eliminate the need for drugs or crime related to drug abuse and illegal sales (Goldkamp, 2000; Hora, Schma, Rosenthal, 1999; "Looking at a Decade," 1998). In so doing, drug treatment courts represent a practical application of the theoretical concept of *therapeutic jurisprudence*, wherein the judicial system is used primarily for "healing" rather than punitive purposes (Wexler & Winick, 1996).

The earliest drug courts were established by a small network cf committed public officials, judges, court administrators, treatment providers, prosecutors, and criminal defense attorneys who shared their experiences and newfound expertise, who traveled to one another's courts at their own expense to observe and/or to provide assistance (Goldkamp, 2000). These drug courts were the product of local innovation and hard work and, as a rule, produced new initiatives with broad-based support from local justice officials but typically operated with very little (usually locally-generated) funding (Goldkamp, 2000). The success of these initial programs in due time lead to substantial federal funding and the expansion of the number of drug courts to approximately 2,193 operating in all fifty states (Bureau of Justice Statistics Drug Court Clearinghouse, 2011).

Program achievements have generally included lower recidivism rates for graduates than found with other drug offenders and cost savings realized for taxpayers. The results from cost evaluations of 20 Oregon drug courts showed an average 3-year outcome cost savings of $6,812 per drug court participant when compared to similar simulated offender profiles processed through the criminal justice system, but who did not enter a drug court. When victimizations are included, the outcome cost savings over 3 years increase from $6,812 per participant to $16,933 per participant (Carey & Waller, 2011, p. 74).

A study of seven Maryland Adult Drug Treatment Court Programs found a 29% reduction in new arrests (over 2 years from program entry). Cost evaluations for the Maryland drug courts showed an average 24-month cost savings of $1,982 per drug court participant as compared to offenders who were eligible for drug court but who chose not to participate (Mackin et al., 2009, p. 61). (See Rossman, Roman, Zweig, Rempel, & Lindquist, 2011 for a seven state adult drug court outcome evaluation. Also see Rempel et al., 2003); Barnowski & Aos, 2003; Turley & Sibley, 2001; Brewster, 2001; and; Judicial Council of California, 2002 for similar findings in New York, Washington, Texas, Pennsylvania, and California respectively).

These findings prompted the federal government to finance these programs on a consistent basis. The positive outcomes and financial support for felony drug court clients prompted dependency court judges to re-examine their approach to child abuse and neglect cases, and the growing number of drug-involved parents.

Family Drug Treatment Courts

Family drug treatment courts oversee cases involving adult substance abusers who face the threat of loss or restriction of their parental rights by the state, arising out of their substance use. The goal of the family drug court is to treat the substance-abusing parent so that the family can be reunited and the family unit sustained (McGee, Merrigan, Parnham, & Smith, 2000, p. 3).

Before the crack epidemic began in the early 1980s, child protective service matters typically dealt with either lapses in parental supervision or educational neglect. When crack hit the streets, however, the number of neglect filings virtually skyrocketed and the character of the cases brought before the family court changed radically. Besharov (1990) reported that a review of foster care in New York City showed costs rose from $320 million in 1985 to $795 million by 1991 (attributing most of the cost to the crack epidemic effects on families). Toufexis (1991, p. 57) observed that during this same time-frame, the use of crack cocaine became widespread, and the annual placements of drug-affected babies increased from 750 to approximately 3,500 by 1991. No longer did cases concern allegations of poor housekeeping or parental inattention. Drug addiction and its attendant ills – crime, sickness, total family dysfunction – became the more routine allegations that arose in this time period and that continue today.

National government estimates hold that drug abuse either causes or contributes to seven of ten cases of child maltreatment (National Center on Addiction and Substance Abuse, 1999, p. 4). A 2008 study by Osterling and Austin estimated parental substance use to affect 50% – 80% of families with child welfare services involvement.

The National Center on Child Abuse Prevention Research (2001) found 85% of states reported that substance abuse was one of the two major problems (the other being poverty) exhibited by families in which maltreatment was suspected. The Child Welfare League (1998) reported an estimated 67% of parents in the child welfare system required substance abuse treatment services, but child welfare agencies were able to provide treatment for fewer than 1/3 of these families. Furthermore, in most states the waiting period for treatment services was up to 12 months.

The lack of adequate substance abuse treatment services for parents is a major obstacle to family reunification in child welfare cases. In addition to removing children from parents due to neglect arising out of drug use, massive arrests from the "War on Drugs" separated drug-involved parents from many children through incarceration (Tupper, 2005).

Much like the rest of the legal community, dependency court judges took notice of the positive outcomes the early drug courts were achieving with their clients. In 1994, Reno, Nevada became the first family court to apply felony drug court methods to cases where parents became involved in a civil child protection case due to their substance abuse (McGee, et al., 2000). Intensive, continuous judicial supervision of participants and coordination of treatment and rehabilitation services were offered to families whose unity was threatened by parental drug use. Although similar to the adult drug courts in terms of services and protocols, family drug courts generally focus most consistently on the "best interests of the child." This focus is the court's paramount consideration in responding to the progress (or regression) of the parent who is engaged with the court. Missing scheduled visits with their children, continued relationships with (substance) using friends, or inability to secure safe and sober housing can cause a parent to lose custody of their children. Each of these indictors is believed to be a reliable predictor of 'using' behavior, thus putting the parents' children at continued risk of an unsafe home environment.

As noted above few published studies exist on the efficacy of family treatment courts. The rare evaluations conducted to date have, however, generally reported promising outcomes for families. Out of 115 individuals who entered the Suffolk County program from January 1998 through April 2000, only 15 were terminated for being unsuccessful in accomplishing favorable behavior change ("Confronting the Cycle," 2000). The retention rate for a study published in 2000 of 14 family treatment courts was over 75%, and the average rate of failed drug tests for all participants was 12%, as compared to a 30% average for respondents in traditional family courts ("Family Drug Court Activity Update," 2000). Of special note is Simpson & Sells 1982 report, citing four national studies, spanning the period from 1968 to 1995 that assessed approximately 70,000 patients. One of the major findings of each study was that the length of time a patient spent in treatment was a reliable predictor of his or her post-treatment performance (See also Hubbard, Craddock, & Anderson, 2003, and Simpson & Flynn, 2008 regarding national follow-up treatment outcome studies finding length of treatment positively correlates with improved post-treatment outcomes). A five-county family drug treatment court comparative study found children reached permanent placement three months sooner, had a permanent plan ordered five months earlier, and had their CPS case closed four months sooner than the comparison groups (Young, 2005).

As with the prison cost savings that can be realized in felony drug court, savings in reduced foster care can provide a significant financial benefit directly attributable to the family treatment court approach ("Confronting the Cycle," 2000). A 2008 evaluation of the Baltimore

City Family Recovery Program (FRP) found that because FRP families utilized less foster care and were more likely to achieve reunification, FRP cases were less costly to the child welfare system than other Child in Need of Assistance (CINA) cases. Thus, the total net cost savings per year of Baltimore City FRP operations was nearly $1,004,456 or approximately $5,022 per served family. (Burrus, Mackin, & Aborn, 2008).

In 2000, the average foster care stay for a child in New York City, who did not have any special needs, was approximately four years – costing $15,200 per year, per child ("Confronting the Cycle," 2000). The average foster care stay for a child whose parent is successfully treated in the Manhattan Family Treatment Court is only eleven months. Thus, a rough estimate of the cost savings attributable to the Manhattan Family Treatment Court approach is nearly $45,000 per child. By comparison, the Washington State Department of Social and Health Services Children's Administration spent an average of $1,578 per month for each child in state foster care in 2005. (The cost for special needs children is approximately four times that amount.) ("Report to the Legislature," 2006, p. 6).

Family treatment courts can also result in medical care cost savings. A 2004 study conducted by the Washington State Department of Health and Social Services, Research and Data Analysis Division found significant medical cost savings associated with chemical dependency treatment for Supplemental Security Income (SSI) clients (Nordlund, 2004). The average monthly emergency room cost was $442 for SSI clients who needed chemical dependency treatment but did not receive it. These costs were reduced to $288 per month for SSI clients who receive chemical dependency treatment – an ER cost offset of $154 per client, per month. This represents a 35% reduction in average monthly ER-related medical costs for SSI clients who receive chemical dependency treatment, compared to SSI clients who need, but do not receive, chemical dependency treatment.

Another indication of parents' success in sobriety is permanent reunification with their children. Multiple studies have found that parents who participate in a family treatment court are significantly more likely to be reunified with their children than were matched non-participants. A report on the Thurston County, Washington, Family Treatment Court published in 2005 found that 75% of the eighty-two children served from March 2000 to October 2003 either had been placed with the birth family or were pending return to the birth family

(U.S. Department of Justice, 2005, p. 16). In June 2000, fourteen family treatment courts around the country (out of a total nineteen in operation at the time) reported that 60% of their clients had either remained with their children or were reunited with them ("Family Drug Court Activity," 2000). Results such as these have prompted a rapid growth of family treatment courts (Also see Marlowe, 2011; Dakof, et. al., 2010; Worcel, Furrer, Green, Burrus, & Finigan (2008), for positive correlation findings between family treatment court participation and family reunification). As of July 2010, two hundred sixty-five family drug courts were in operation in thirty-seven states, (BJA Drug Court Clearinghouse Project, 2010).[1] The following section outlines the research theory and study objectives for one of those family drug courts.

---

[1] It is interesting to note the state-to-state disparity regarding number of operational family treatment courts. For example, Washington has 16 family treatment courts, while Idaho has 2, and Oregon, 8. More populous states such as Texas has 5 FTCs in operation, California - 15, Florida – 23, and New York - 55. The following ten states have no family treatment courts in operation: AR, CT, DE, IL, KS, KY, LA, MA, MS, NH, ND, SD and WV. However, several of these states have unified juvenile/family courts.

CHAPTER 2

Parental Addiction and Recovery: The Life Course Theory

Individuals in this study are examined through the theoretical lens of Sampson and Laub's (1993) Life Course Theory of deviant behavior. Sampson and Laub's theory postulates a central role for social bonds as preventative of social deviance, asserting that the quality of social bonds, which they describe as the basis for the exercise of informal social control, helps to explain the onset, persistence, and desistence from deviant behavior (p. 21).

Life course theory has four guiding principles:

1. Lives are lived interdependently.
2. Individuals construct their life courses within a set of social constraints.
3. The developmental impact of life events depends on their timing in life.
4. The individual life course is embedded in historical time and place (Elder, Jr. 1998).

The two main concepts in Sampson and Laub's (1993) theory are *life trajectories* (pathways of development over the life span, such as work life, marital status or parenthood), and *transitions* (life events, such as first job or first marriage, that are embedded in trajectories and evolve over shorter time spans, p. 8). Life course theorist Glen H. Elder, Jr. (1985, p. 31) describes these transitions thusly: "changes that are more or less abrupt," noting that the interlocking nature of trajectories and transitions may generate *turning points* or a noteworthy or lasting change in the life course. According to Sampson and Laub (2003), involvement in institutions such as marriage, work, and the military can serve as turning points for many people by reordering short-term situational inducements to crime and, over time, redirecting long-term commitments to conformity. What appears to be important about institutional or structural turning points is that they all involve, to varying degrees (pp. 148-9):

1. New situations that "knife off" the past from the present
2. New situations that provide both supervision and monitoring as well as new opportunities of social support and growth
3. New situations that change and structure routine activities
4. New situations that provide the opportunity for identity transformation

Sampson and Laub (2005) revised their theory to feature the importance of human agency in accessing or declining turning points that present themselves over the adult life course. They noted in this respect the following:

> Human agency cannot be divorced from the situation or context, making choice situated or relational, rather than a property of the person or even the environment. Life course criminology has been remiss to have left agency—which is essentially human social action—largely out of the theoretical picture. We seek to reposition human agency as a central element in understanding crime and deviance over the life course (pp. 38-9).

Life course theorist Glen Elder, Jr. (1985, p. 35) notes, "Adaptation to life events is crucial because the same event or transition followed by different adaptations can lead to different trajectories." People bring a life history of personal experiences and dispositions to each transition, interpret the new circumstances in terms of this history, and work out lines of adaptation that can fundamentally alter their life course (Elder, Jr., 1998, p. 957).

The discovery of life course as a sociological analytical construct is widely attributed to William Thomas and Florian Znaniecki (1918), whose pioneering study on cultural identity and social change in the Polish immigrant community in early twentieth century America sought to explain social problems by examining the relationship between individuals and their surrounding society. Like Sampson and Laub, Thomas and Znaniecki recognized the integral nature of human agency to life course theory, stating, "An attitude as manifested in an isolated act is always subject to misinterpretation, but this danger diminishes in the very measure of our ability to connect this act with past acts of the same individual" (Vol. 3, p. 7). Thomas spent more than a decade collecting oral reports and written materials in the Chicago Polish community, and later through a liaison with Znaniecki, in Poland. By utilizing a variety of documents ranging from newspaper reports, organizational archives, to personal letters and diaries as ethnographic sources, Thomas was able to develop the biographic approach in sociology. In advocating this approach Thomas and Znaniecki noted, "It is clear that even for the characterization of single social data – attitudes and values – personal life-records give us the most exact approach" (Thomas & Znaniecki, 1918: Vol. 3, p. 7).

Beginning in the 1930s, and for the ensuing forty years, Sheldon and Eleanor Glueck conducted crime and delinquency research at Harvard University using a methodological approach similar to Thomas and Znaniecki's cultural identity and social change studies. Like Thomas and Znaniecki, the Gluecks stressed the importance of collecting multiple sources of information (e.g., parent, teacher, self-reports) in addition to official records in longitudinal studies. (Sampson & Laub, 1993, p. 35).

In the 1960s, life course theory extended from child delinquency studies into the adult years of the study subjects (Elder, 1998, p. 940). The extension of the early child samples to the adult years provided impetus to the scientific study of adult development, and sharpened awareness of the need for a research paradigm that would give proper attention to human development beyond childhood to life trajectories.

By the 1970s and 1980s, life course studies began focusing on adolescent to adulthood timeframes, and young to middle adulthood. Researchers Thornberry and Krohn (2003, p. 317) identified key findings emerging from many of these contemporary longitudinal studies pertaining to the causes, course, and consequences of delinquency and criminal activity:

1. Effective parenting (defined as monitoring and supervision of children) early in life yields more positive outcomes among

offspring, and; there is an intergenerational transmission of [deviance].

2. Antisocial and criminal activity impact other aspects of an individual's life, such as parental behavior, educational attainment, childbearing, mate selection, and so forth.
3. The life course transitions of marriage and grade retention can alter crime trajectories (marriage decreases deviant tendencies; grade retention (i.e., repeating a grade) increases them) (Laub, Nagin, & Sampson, 1998; Nagin, Pagani, Tremblay, & Vitaro, 2003).

Numerous studies exist on life course theory, demonstrating its applicability to desistence from crime (See Schroeder, Giordano & Cernkovich, 2007; Doherty, 2006; Benda, 2005; O'Connell, 2003), and variations in alcohol or substance use over the life course. In their study on baby boomer heroin and methamphetamine users, Boeri, Sterk, & Elifson (2006) used analytical tools from a life course perspective concluding:

> First, the focus on mainstream social roles as required in social control theory was too narrow and, second, the dichotomous perspective of self-control theory was too restrictive to adequately explain the drug use patterns in our sample. We soon realized the need for a more complex model to effectively evaluate drug users that would include the genuine diversity of drug use phases (p. 271).

The authors concluded that social roles and self-control were related to turning points and transitions in the drug career over the life course (p. 281), finding that attachment to and involvement in social roles, such as employment, helped the user maintain control over their drug use at various stages of his/her life.

In her study of homeless, substance-abusing men, Hartwell (2003) found consistent patterns of non-normative social ties and the accumulation of unconventional social capital that lead to the men remaining deviant across the life course (p. 497). She concluded that changes must be made at both structural and social service system levels to alter the life course of these men entrenched in their social role (as substance abusers) due to both personal and institutional experiences. Structural changes included extended treatment courses, living wage jobs, access to and use of relevant social and health services (p. 498).

Nielson (1999) used data from the 1991 National Household Survey on Drug Abuse (NHSDA) to examine background and social bonding variables associated with fewer intoxications. She found being female, higher education levels and higher family income were background variables associated with fewer times drunk. The social bond variables associated with fewer occasions of drunkenness were those of either being employed or being a homemaker. Marriage was associated with fewer times drunk relative to being single, and being separated or divorced was associated with more frequent drunkenness than being married or single. Being a parent, however, had no impact on the number of times drunk (p. 143).

This research asserts that the life course theory framework is highly applicable to families where parents are drug-dependent, and whose dependence results in child maltreatment. Most of the parents in the FTC families were themselves raised in chaotic homes where familial and friendship relationships were transitory, and wherein substance use was a staple. The majority of clients learned from childhood through the example of adults in their lives that controlled substances – be it alcohol, tobacco, over-the-counter, prescription, or illicit drugs – were the principal means required to socialize, to cope with stress, or even to function on a daily basis.[2] As these individuals reached adolescence and continued into adulthood, their life trajectory predictably continued on a path where their friendships and partner choices centered around substance use. As such, the pathways of many of these individuals were destined for relational discord, delinquency, educational disinvestment, disengagement from emotional, financial, and intellectual problems and solutions, by seeking and acquiring a steady supply of mind-altering substances that only served to hinder their cognitive, social and emotional maturation processes.[3]

The transition into puberty and adulthood also brings with it a new twist – reproductive ability – which greatly complicates the drug-

---

[2] At program entry, 69% of FTC clients reported a family history of chemical dependency. The majority (mode) of FTC clients began using drugs by age 12.

[3] Forty percent of FTC clients completed less than a high school education at program entry; another 45% had only a high school diploma or GED. Clients self-reported a total of 54 arrests in the year prior to program entry. They also reported being charged 173 times with a total of 382 criminal charges, ranging from homicide to property crimes over their lifetime.

dependent or addicted individual's life through the potential (indeed likelihood) of pregnancy. Jones (1999, p. 14) reported a higher incidence of pregnancy among drug addicts due to their high frequency of sexual bartering and poor contraceptive practices, noting, "Typically, drug addicts are not practicing any type of family planning or, in the alternative, birth control." Oberman (1992, p. 18) observed that the majority of drug-dependent women in her study reported incidents of previous sexual abuse, and that the resulting low self-esteem made it difficult to refuse unwanted sexual advances or to insist on the use of contraception when engaging in sexual relations. Many drug addicts exchange sex for drugs, thus refusal of sex jeopardizes their drug supply. Whereas in healthy, trusting, sober relationships an individual can turn to those closest to them for support and solutions to problems, the isolation and chaos inherent in drug-dependent lifestyles offers few if any resources for one to extract themselves from the only way of life they know.

When becoming a parent does not provide a transition from a drug-dependent lifestyle to a sober one the state (CPS) must sometimes intervene and serve as a "change point" for these families who desperately want to stay together but who lack the financial, intellectual, social, and emotional tools to overcome the many obstacles they face in achieving that goal. When a parent's life trajectory involving substance abuse leads to the horrifying life event of having their children taken by the state, if provided access to a comprehensive supportive services the troubled parents may be able to change their life trajectory of chaos, substance abuse, and parental neglect to one of sobriety, personal growth, and parental responsibility that potentially provide a transition for their own life trajectories, as well as those of their children.

Under the rubric of Sampson and Laub's (2003, p. 148) theory, family treatment courts have the potential to serve as institutional or structural *turning points*, due to their ability to provide a new situation that: 1) "knives off" the past from the present; 2) provides both supervision and monitoring as well as new opportunities of social support and growth; 3) change in and productive structure of routine activities, and; 4) provides the opportunity for identity transformation. Such an intervention can serve as a life transition that intersects with a life trajectory spiraling down into more severe and destructive drug use, and redirect parents' life trajectory towards sobriety and family reunification. Alternatively, it may only serve as a brief interruption in a unidirectional life trajectory that leads to the termination of parental rights as the parent continues down the same drug-dependent path.

The Family Treatment Court as Turning Point

Professor Andrew Abbott (1997, p. 89) contends, "What makes a turning point a turning point rather than a minor ripple is the passage of sufficient time 'on a new course' such that it becomes clear that direction has indeed been changed." Because the family treatment court provides a greater scope and duration of services never before experienced by parents whose children were removed by the state due to parental drug use, the expectation by FTC team members is that this program can serve as a change point that can lead participants to different trajectories than did previous treatment programs (e.g., sobriety, family reunification, stable housing and income).

The traditional dependency system, with its mandated periodic judicial reviews, does not provide a meaningful or motivating consequence for the non-complying parent (McGee, et al., 2000, p. 20). Prior to the establishment of the family treatment court in the jurisdiction under study, families who were CPS-involved due to substance abuse were typically required to enter a chemical dependency treatment program, which usually resulted in a placement on a 3-month waiting list. For families who continued to choose this option, this referral was generally followed by state-approved funding for a 90-day outpatient treatment program (least restrictive environment [i.e., least expensive from the state's perspective]) that provided only addiction treatment services. It is common practice to require clients to fail at an outpatient level of care before the state will pay for an inpatient program. This benefit can only be realized if the client is still willing to attend a more rigorous level of treatment after having just failed a less rigorous one. Inpatient programs provide a minimum twenty-eight days of intensive treatment, generally followed by the client's return to an outpatient program for two to three months.

In the typical outpatient treatment program, any issues a client faces outside of their addiction but that can clearly affect their sobriety (e.g., mental health issues, unemployment, homelessness, dental or other physical health issues), are essentially not addressed in treatment. Few programs are gender-specific, and even fewer address the unique circumstances faced by parents who are drug-dependent and in danger of losing custody of their children. Should the client complete this six-month process (only half of which is spent in actual treatment) without any delays or setbacks, they then report back to dependency court six months after their children were removed (their children may or may not be in their care during this time, but they likely have visitation with their children). If they are adjudged to be progressing in their sobriety, they report to dependency court four to six months later, during which time their only available sobriety support is that provided by Narcotics Anonymous groups – gatherings where many recovering addicts feel at the greatest risk of relapse in their efforts to remain sober.

Over half of FTC clients had previously entered abbreviated substance abuse treatment programs such as these. Of those, more than half successfully graduated from the programs in question. However, the vast majority (nearly 89%) of FTC clients reported the longest period they were ever able to maintain sobriety during their lives was two years. Particularly as a parent, sobriety must be maintained for a much longer period. An extended treatment course such as the FTC yearlong program has the potential to achieve more than sobriety, measured by clean UAs and consistent community meeting attendance.

A yearlong program also allows enough time for a parent to make difficult life decisions after a longer duration of sobriety when they are better able to make them. McGee (2000) accurately summarizes, "Given the compelling nature of addiction and the debilitating influence on the user's ability to appreciate the long-term consequences of their use, termination of parental rights often appears to be a vague process "to be dealt with" several months in the future. Addiction denies the parent appropriate foresight and forces the addict to live and survive only for the moment. Future threats, regardless of their severity do not motivate the drug dependent individual" (p. 20). The opportunity afforded to parents via an family treatment court to build social capital in sober social circles is a key element in Sampson and Laub's Life Course Theory, and essential in improving client outcomes post-program (Coleman, 1988).

The Importance of Social Capital in Recovery and Reunification

Putnam (2000) succinctly describes social capital as "connections among individuals – social networks and the norms of reciprocity and trustworthiness that arise from them." Sampson and Laub (1993) assert that these interpersonal connections discourage individuals from engaging in deviant behavior. Because such interpersonal connections take time to develop, it is unlikely that a 28-day inpatient or 90-day outpatient treatment program can provide an adequate timeframe in which to transition a person in crisis whose life and relationships revolve around drug use, to a person with a sober social network.

Further, it is more difficult to connect with people who are not experiencing the same consequences of their drug use (e.g., possible loss of a child) in a typical outpatient treatment program. If given twelve to fourteen months, however, to develop trusting relationships with a judge, a treatment counselor, a CWS worker, a family preservation specialist, a family counselor – all of whom are willing to advocate for you and support your hard work in recovery – as well as the opportunity to build relationships with other parents who share your same burdens and who are willing to do the difficult work of an intensive outpatient recovery program with you, there is an opportunity to change a person's view, to show them another way, and to support them while they test their abilities to navigate this new, unfamiliar life trajectory.

Hypotheses

Due to the extended treatment course of the family treatment court and the potential to redirect a life trajectory as put forth in the Life Course Theory framework, it is hypothesized here that:

H1: Clients who participate in the family treatment court will have a higher family reunification rate than non-participants.

H2: Clients who participate in the family treatment court will be re-referred to CPS less frequently than non-participants, once their FTC dependency is dismissed.

H3: Clients who participate in the family treatment court will remain clean and sober for longer periods than non-participants.

H4: Clients who participate in the family treatment court will retain stable employment for longer periods than non-participants.

H5: Clients who participate in the family treatment court will establish permanent housing for longer periods than non-participants.

H6: Clients who participate in the family treatment court will attain higher education levels than non-participants.

Empirical support for these six hypotheses would indicate that the FTC program serves as an effective agent of therapeutic jurisprudence by helping the clients of the court change their life course in a positive direction.

CHAPTER 3

Whose Family Is It?

Parental Autonomy and State Sovereignty

As will be discussed below, both the judiciary and the legislature have firmly established parents' constitutionally recognized right to raise their children as they see fit in accordance with their beliefs, values and lifestyles without undue governmental interference. It is equally well established that parental autonomy in child rearing is not absolute, and that the sovereign states have the power to intervene coercively in the lives of families for the purpose of protecting minor children from maltreatment (Gittler, 2003; RCW 13.34.020). This most private of social institutions has established itself as a central focus of heightened constitutional concern in a line of cases affirming the importance of the family as a fundamental social unit.

The U.S. Supreme Court has frequently emphasized the importance of the family in its jurisprudence. In *Meyer* v. *Nebraska* (1923) the Supreme Court first recognized a constitutional right of childrearing. The Court held that a Nebraska statute making it unlawful to teach any languages other than English to children before the eighth grade was determined to violate the liberty right of parents inherent in the Fourteenth Amendment to bring up their children. The Court held, "the state should [not] entirely usurp the parent's role, providing common guardianship, such that "no parent is to know his own child ...." (p. 262).

In *Pierce v. Society of Sisters* (1925), the Court struck down an Oregon statute requiring nearly all children between the ages of eight and sixteen to attend public schools, in effect outlawing private and home schooling at that level. In invalidating the statute, the Court cited the "doctrine of *Meyer*" that there is a "liberty of parents and guardians to direct the upbringing and education of children under their control" (534). Justice McReynolds invoked the specter of the all-enveloping government, insisting that the "child is not the mere creature of the state" (535).

In *Prince v. Massachusetts* (1944), the Court held that the guarantee of "liberty" under the Due Process Clause of the Fourteenth Amendment preserves a "private realm of family life which the state cannot enter" [166].[4] The high court has also upheld the sanctity of the family under the Equal Protection Clause of the Fourteenth Amendment. In *Stanley v. Illinois* (1972), the Court held an Illinois statute unconstitutional that declared children of unmarried fathers as dependent (i.e., wards of the state) without a hearing on parental fitness and without proof of neglect. "We have concluded that all Illinois parents are constitutionally entitled to a hearing on their fitness before their children are removed from their custody. It follows that denying such a hearing to Stanley and those like him (unmarried fathers) while granting it to other Illinois parents is inescapably contrary to the Equal Protection Clause." "[A] natural parent who has demonstrated sufficient commitment to his or her children is thereafter entitled to raise the children free from undue state interference" (649).

Further, in *Finnerty v. Boyett* (1985), the Court recognized a natural father's right under the Fourteenth Amendment guarantees of an opportunity to develop a relationship with his children. In addition to delineating between state and family control of children, the family also provides a useful boundary to restrict an otherwise broad scope of individual liberties, when exercised within the family sphere. For example, Washington State Constitution Article I, Section 7 - Invasion of Private Affairs or Home Prohibited states, "No person shall be disturbed in his private affairs, or his home invaded, without authority of law."

Conversely, in *Bowers v. Hardwick* (1986), the Court held that the Constitution does not "reach so far" as to protect individual privacy independent of family relations (191). The family can be an instrument

---

[4] The Court also noted however, that, "The family itself is not beyond regulation in the public interest." (The Court ruled that the state could intervene and overrule a parent's decision to violate child labor laws by requiring children to peddle religious materials on the street as a family.)

of individual liberty only when the interests of the individual and the family unit are in harmony. The conflict between family and individual privacy becomes manifest the moment individuals within the family disagree over fundamental issues of personal life (parental drug use vs. parenting), and they seek, or the state requires, public adjudication of their internal disagreement (Daily, 1993). The principle of individual sovereignty demands a family be open to public scrutiny at certain times, particularly when the well-being of a child is at issue. The state has the authority to remove a drug-dependent parent's child from their home, impose a treatment plan on the parent, and refuse to return the children to the parent's care if said parent continues to violate their treatment plan. (See RCW 13.34.176 Violation of Alcohol or Substance Abuse Treatment Conditions — Hearing — Notice — Modification of order (2):

> If the court finds that there has been a violation of the treatment conditions it shall modify the dependency order, as necessary, to ensure the safety of the child. The modified order shall remain in effect until the party is in full compliance with the treatment requirements.

At one time, most state statutes did not require a showing of a causal relationship between specified parental conduct and harm to a child as a prerequisite for coercive state intervention designed to protect a child from abuse and neglect. Beginning in the mid-1970's, however, these statutes increasingly became the object of critical scrutiny. As the Juvenile Justice Standards Project's Standards Relating to Abuse and Neglect (1981) stated:

> These statutes appear to assume that we can tell whether a child is endangered, and intervention is appropriate, solely on the basis of parental conduct. This assumption is contrary to the available social science evidence which indicates that it is very difficult or impossible to correlate parental behavior to specific detriment to the child. Studies have amply demonstrated that even our most sophisticated techniques of predicting long-range harm to children on the basis of particular parental behavior are woefully inadequate. Since prediction is so difficult, the danger of over intervention, i.e., intervention harmful to the child is increased by focusing

solely on parental behavior. Moreover, there is substantial evidence that intervention often occurs in situations where there is no demonstrable harm to the child and no strong likelihood of harm occurring.

As a result of criticism of state statutes regarding child abuse and neglect authorizing intervention solely on the basis of parental conduct, many of these statutes were amended to make a showing of specific harm or likelihood of harm to a child a prerequisite for state intervention (Gittler, 2003). For example, Wash. Rev. Code Ann. § 26.44.170(1) Alleged child abuse or neglect — Use of alcohol or controlled substances as contributing factor — Evaluation states:

> (1)When, as a result of a report of alleged child abuse or neglect, an investigation is made that includes an in-person contact with the person who is alleged to have committed the abuse or neglect, there shall be a determination of whether it is probable that the use of alcohol or controlled substances is a contributing factor to the alleged abuse or neglect.
>
> (3) If a determination is made under subsection (1) of this section that there is probable cause to believe abuse of alcohol or controlled substances has contributed to the child abuse or neglect, the department shall, within available funds, cause a comprehensive chemical dependency evaluation to be made of the person or persons so identified. The evaluation shall be conducted by a physician or persons certified under rules adopted by the department to make such evaluation. The department shall perform the duties assigned under this section within existing personnel resources.

State statutes use a variety of terms to refer to child maltreatment that warrant coercive state intervention. The terms "abuse" and "neglect" are often used to denote such maltreatment. Although statutory definitions of these terms vary somewhat, "abuse" typically is defined as parental acts that harm a child or create a risk of harm to a child, and "neglect" is typically defined as parental omissions to act that are harmful to a child or create a risk of harm to a child (Gittler, 2003). Statutory definitions of abuse and neglect delineating the authority of juvenile and family courts and child welfare authorities to coercively intervene on behalf of abused and neglected children are a matter of state law.

The Child Abuse Prevention and Treatment Act (CAPTA), 42 U.S.C. 5106g (2001), requires states receiving federal funding for child abuse prevention and treatment activities to incorporate certain minimum elements in their statutory definitions of abuse and neglect. This legislation, as amended, provides that child abuse and neglect "means at a minimum, any recent act or failure to act on the part of a parent or caretaker, which results in death, serious physical or emotional harm, sexual abuse or exploitation, or an act or failure to act which presents serious risk of imminent harm" (2). Washington Administrative Code (WAC) 388-15-009:

> (5) Negligent treatment or maltreatment means an act or a failure to act on the part of a child's parent, legal custodian, guardian, or caregiver that shows a serious disregard of the consequences to the child of such magnitude that it creates a clear and present danger to the child's health, welfare, and safety. A child does not have to suffer actual damage or physical or emotional harm to be in circumstances which create a clear and present danger to the child's health, welfare, and safety. Negligent treatment or maltreatment includes, but is not limited, to:
>
>> (a) Failure to provide adequate food, shelter, clothing, supervision, or health care necessary for a child's health, welfare, and safety. Poverty and/or homelessness do not constitute negligent treatment or maltreatment in and of themselves;
>> (b) Actions, failures to act, or omissions that result in injury to or which create a substantial risk of injury to the physical, emotional, and/or cognitive development of a child; or
>> (c) The cumulative effects of consistent inaction or behavior by a parent or guardian in providing for the physical, emotional and developmental needs of a child, or the effects of chronic failure on the part of a parent or guardian to perform basic parental functions, obligations, and duties, when the result is to cause injury or create a

substantial risk of injury to the physical, emotional, and/or cognitive development of a child.

When a court adjudicates a child to be abused or neglected, it has several dispositional alternatives. These alternatives range from allowing the child to remain in his or her home with in-home monitoring and services, to the placement of the child in foster care or other out-of-home placement. For the parents accused of abuse and neglect of their children, civil actions include contempt for not complying with family reunification court order, loss of child custody, and termination of parental rights. Parents may also be subject to criminal prosecution for abuse and neglect of their children (Gittler, 2003; RCW 9A.42 Series). The advent of family treatment courts in 1994, however, appeared to suggest policy support for family unification as did federal legislation passed three years later. This federal statute (discussed below) requires states to establish permanency plans for children more quickly than in the past. Yet in effect, this well-intentioned legislation made it extremely difficult for parents who struggled with drug dependence to regain custody of their children.

Adoption and Safe Families Act (ASFA)

In the past, the welfare system gave parents generous timeframes to complete a reunification plan and regain custody of their children. Courts and social service agencies worked under the premise that it is advantageous for families to remain together, if at all possible. Prevailing wisdom was, and still is to a large extent, that family unity enhances children's developmental health, solidifies their ability to bond to others, and provides parents with a tangible incentive to improve. Ryan, Marsh, Testa, & Louderman (2006) assert that family reunification remains a state child welfare goal primarily because it "respects the primacy of parent-child attachments and the role of the biological family in human connectedness" (96). A typical plan might include requirements that parents complete a drug treatment program, attend parenting classes, and provide a stable residence for their children. In 1997, however, child welfare advocates who had become frustrated with the slow progress of drug-using parents supported the enactment of the federal statute entitled the "Adoption and Safe Families Act" (ASFA). ASFA requires that a permanency hearing to determine a child's permanent placement be held 12 months after a child enters foster care (starting from the date of adjudication or 60 days from the child's removal from the home, whichever is earlier), or within 30 days of a formal determination that no reasonable efforts to preserve or reunite the family are required by child welfare advocates. At most, this leaves fourteen months for a parent to succeed under an established case plan before a permanency plan must be determined (Earp, 2004, p. 37).

The permanency hearing involves significantly more than a review or an extension of placement. The hearing must determine the permanency plan for the child. Under federal regulations, the court must determine whether and when the child will be:

- Returned to the parent
- Placed for adoption, with the agency filing a termination of parental rights (TPR) petition
- Placed permanently with a fit and willing relative
- Referred for legal guardianship
- Placed in another planned permanent living arrangement (this final option is to be taken only in cases in which the agency has documented a compelling reason that none of the first four options would be in the child's best interest).

ASFA requires that a child protection agency file or join a TPR petition when a child under its protection has been in foster care for 15 of the past 22 months; the court determines that the child has been abandoned; or the court, following ASFA guidelines, determines that no reasonable efforts to preserve or reunite the family are required. There are three exceptions to the TPR requirements:

- The child is being cared for by a relative.
- The agency has documented compelling reasons that TPR would not be in the best interest of the child.
- The agency has not provided necessary services in a period consistent with the case plan (in cases where reasonable efforts are required) (p. 38).
- ASFA does mandate that child welfare agencies make "reasonable efforts" to preserve or reunite families. Specifically, the agencies must make reasonable efforts to:

- Prevent the initial removal of a child from his or her home (this applies only when keeping the family together does not endanger the health and safety of the child).
- Make it possible for a child who has been taken from the home to reunite with his or her parents (such efforts may occur during only the 12 months from the date the child entered foster care unless compelling reasons exist to extend the limit).

If reuniting a child with his or her parents is no longer the goal, the child welfare agency must place the child in a permanent, safe, and nurturing home. Reasonable efforts to preserve or reunite the family are not needed when any of the following circumstances exist:

- A child has been subjected to "aggravated circumstances" as defined by state law (e.g., abandonment, torture, chronic abuse, or sexual abuse).
- A parent has aided or abetted, attempted, conspired, solicited, or committed the murder or voluntary manslaughter of another of his or her children.
- A parent has committed a felony assault resulting in serious bodily injury to the child or to another of his or her children.
- A parent's rights to another child have been involuntarily terminated (p. 37).

The characteristics of the family treatment court have great potential in helping meet ASFA accelerated timeframes and goals. The accountability by the parent, service providers, and the court, and the reduced duplication of services that are characteristic of family treatment courts all further the goal of safely returning children to their families or finding permanent placements for children who cannot return home (p. 36). One FTC treatment team member observed:

> We're better able to meet the mandatory AFSA timelines with FTC because clients are able to get right into treatment and we can gauge how they're doing before they've even had their first hearing.

To meet ASFA timelines, the Department of Social and Health Services follows the permanency planning schedule listed below for parents involved in a dependency (RCW 13.34.145). One of the treatment team CWS workers summarized:

- A fact-finding must be held within 45 days of the shelter care hearing.
- A status review is held six months after placement. Child welfare workers inform the judge of the child and parent status during the first six months of placement.
- A permanency review is held nine to twelve months after placement. Child welfare must inform the judge what the department's plan is for the family (i.e., reunification, foster-adopt, guardianship, termination.)
- At 15 months, child welfare must file the permanency plan with the court.
- At 18 months, child welfare must have accomplished the permanency plan.

For FTC clients, they are seen in treatment court every other week in the first eighteen weeks of their program, and monthly thereafter, and have attended at least one dependency review hearing (all with the same judge) before the 6-month status review hearing. Non-FTC clients are generally on their own for six months at a time (RCW 13.34.138). Several FTC team members note that by then, it is typically too late to help a family get back on track if the parents continue to use drugs during that time. One AAG notes:

> The problem in the regular dependency system is the long lag time (six months) between when things start to go south and when some form of intervention takes place. I like the immediacy of the whole FTC team dealing with problems.

Family treatment courts can be highly effective in achieving the goals of the ASFA legislation (listed below):

- To ensure safety for abused and neglected children
- To accelerate permanent placements of children
- To increase accountability of the child welfare system

- To promote permanency for children in foster care

CHAPTER 4

Issues for the Children of Drug Abusing Parents

Research consistently demonstrates a strong connection between substance abuse and child maltreatment, as well as child psychiatric disorders and substance abuse. In her congressional testimony, Nancy Young, Ph.D. (2005) observed that when parents are "high," they may exhibit poor judgment, confusion, irritability, paranoia, and increased violence; they may fail to provide adequate supervision. A 1993 national study of families whose parents were abusing alcohol found they were almost twice as likely to have a history of allegations of child maltreatment (58.8% had more than one allegation on record) as families without alcohol problems (34.3% had multiple allegations) (National Center on Child Abuse). Similarly, a study published in 1994 found children whose parents were abusing substances were almost three times (2.7) more likely to be abused and more than four times (4.2) more likely to be neglected than children whose parents were not substance abusers (Kelleher, Chaffin, Hollenberg, & Fischer, 1994). Crandall, Chiu, & Sheehan (2006) found maternal alcohol use as a significant independent risk factor for injury to children in the first year of life – more than twice the national incidence. Chester, Jose, Aldlyami, King, & Moiemen (2006) found parental drug abuse, single parent families, delay to presentation and a lack of first aid were statistically morc prevalent in the "neglect" group of child burn victims than in the "accidental" group. Children in the "neglect" group were also statistically more likely to have deeper burns and require skin grafting. (Also see: Conners, Bradley, Mansell, Liu, Roberts, Burgdorf, et al, 2003; Biederman, 2000; Wilens, & Biederman, 1993; Weintraub, 1990; Earls, Reich, Jung, & Cloninger, 1988).

Consequently, parental substance abuse drives and maintains high child welfare caseloads, often causing families to cycle in and out of the child welfare system with greater frequency than other CPS-involved families.

As the number of cases has soared, child welfare agencies have devoted more resources solely to investigation and foster care, while the provision of services to prevent the recurrence of child maltreatment (i.e., supportive services for parents) has become a lower budget priority. Paradoxically, this drop has occurred as the number of multi-problem families with urgent and complex needs has expanded (Foster & Macchetto, 1999). Interviews with child welfare workers in the FTC revealed, *"We are on our third generation of child neglect cases due to parental substance abuse."*

Parents who abuse alcohol and drugs and maltreat their children usually suffer many problems concurrently. They tend to be socially isolated, live rather chaotic lives, suffer from depression and other chronic health problems, struggle with drained financial resources, and sustaining prolonged unemployment (Bays, 1990, p. 889; Morrison-Dore, M., & Doris, J., 1998). Substance abuse can also ignite a vicious intergenerational cycle of child maltreatment and substance abuse as substance-abusing parents often were once victims of substantial abuse themselves.

Prior to the advent of family treatment courts in 1994, and the 1997 enactment of ASFA, children of substance-abusing parents tended to be placed in foster care more frequently, and stay longer than others in the system ("Children at the Front," 1992, p. 68). In 1999, the National Center on Addiction and Substance Abuse (CASA) proposed the following guiding principles and recommendations to respond to the reality and consequences of a child welfare caseload dominated by substance abusing parents:

1. Every child has a right to have his or her substance-abusing parents get a fair shot at recovery with timely and comprehensive treatment.
2. Every child has a right to be free of drug- and alcohol-abusing parents who are abusing or neglecting them and who refuse to

enter treatment or who, despite treatment, are unable to conquer their abuse and addiction.

3. Every child has a right to have precious and urgent developmental needs take precedence over the timing of parental recovery.
4. The goal of the child welfare system is to form and support safe, nurturing families for children, where possible within the biological family or, where not possible, with an adoptive family (p. 78).

Unfortunately, the number of children adopted out of foster care remains low.

Table 4.1: National Foster Care Placements 1990, 1999 & 2010

Percentage of Children in Foster Care:	**1990^ (Preceding Family Drug Courts)**	**1999* (5-yr Mark for Family Drug Courts)**	**2010~**
Returned to Family of Origin	60%	59%	51%
Lived w/other Family Members or Graduated to Independent Living Arrangements	32%	25%	19%
Adopted	8%	16%**	21%

^(Petit & Curtis, 1997: 69)

* (Evan B. Donaldson Adoption Institute)

~ U.S. Department of Health and Human Services, (2011). *The AFCARS report.*

** The jump in adoption rates can be attributed in large part to the accelerated ASFA timelines enacted in 1997, freeing children for adoption more quickly than before.

In light of these facts, families should be provided with every support service they need in order to rebuild and maintain their family unity in order to avoid multiple involvements at the expense of the state. Family treatment courts are capable of helping drug-using parents achieve sobriety and family reunification, and may be the best opportunity families in these circumstances have to maintain their relationships. For the FTC two-year study period, the 124 study subjects had one hundred ninety-four children residing with someone other than their parents due to parental drug use. Their circumstances seldom respond to simple solutions or quick fixes. Clients having learned as children themselves that the way to deal with conflict or stress is through violence and substance use pass that legacy on to their children until healthy coping mechanisms can replace unhealthy ones.

CHAPTER 5

Issues for Parents in Dependency Due to Drug Use

Parents whose families enter the state child welfare system due to their drug use are afflicted by numerous obstacles, making it difficult to abide by federal family reunification timelines without assistance from intense, comprehensive services. Parents who frequently use drugs are also likely to need parenting training and may have complicating mental or physical health issues. It is quite possible that the parent grew up in a dysfunctional family environment, is the product of multi-generational abuse and neglect, and is, or has been, a victim of domestic violence (Earp, 2004, p. 35). In addition to their drug dependence, many parents suffer from co-occurring mental health issues. Either of these conditions alone or combined hinder parents from maintaining steady employment, which in turn affects parents' ability to acquire permanent housing, dependable childcare, transportation or health care for themselves – all issues they are expected by the state to address in order to regain or retain custody of their children. These multiple challenges frequently go unaddressed by substance abuse treatment providers who hold themselves out as the solution to family reunification. The lack of relevant help for parents whose family unity is threatened by their drug use often feeds into their feelings of self-doubt, and only serves to bolster their continued use to cope with these stressful life circumstances. A discussion of each of these typical obstacles follows.

Co-Occurring Disorders

The Substance Abuse and Mental Health Services Administration (SAMHSA) determined in 2006, that 5 million U.S. adult citizens have a serious mental illness and a co-occurring substance use disorder. Research has found that 73% of persons with a drug dependence disorder in substance abuse treatment had a co-occurring mental disorder at some point during their lifetime (U.S. Department of Health and Human Services, 2009, p. 6). Individuals with co-occurring disorders challenge both clinicians and the treatment delivery system. They most frequently use the costliest services (emergency rooms, inpatient facilities, and outreach intensive services), and often have poor clinical outcomes (Grudzinskas, Clayfield, Roy-Bujnowski, Fisher, & Richardson, 2005, p. 281). A person with co-occurring disorders may abuse one or more of a spectrum of substances and may be diagnosed with one or more mental illnesses. These disorders can result in poor response to traditional treatments and increase the risk for other serious medical problems, often including HIV, Hepatitis B and C, cardiac and pulmonary diseases ("Report to Congress," 2002). If one of the co-occurring disorders goes untreated it can increase the severity of psychiatric symptoms and the likelihood for suicide attempts, violent behaviors, legal, medical and employment problems, and periods of homelessness, separation from families and potentially supportive communities (Grudzinskas, et al., 2005, p. 281).

In Washington State, Shah, et al (2010) analyzed risk factors and outcomes for TANF adults and children over the five-year period from 2005 to 2009. TANF parents with co□occurring conditions were almost three times as likely to be part of a Child Protective Services (CPS) investigation relative to those for whom neither problem was identified (p. 3). Such co□occurring substance abuse and mental illness place children at risk of abuse and neglect.

Historically, individuals with co-occurring disorders received sequential or parallel treatment from the separate mental health services and substance abuse treatment systems. Neither system had developed the capacity to provide both mental health and substance abuse treatment within a single program. Fragmented and uncoordinated services often created a service gap for persons with co-occurring disorders ("Report to Congress," 2002). During the 1980's however, several developments occurred that contributed to a greater focus on the unmet needs of this population, including the following: deinstitutionalization; a younger generation of individuals with mental illness living in the community with access to treatment drugs; and, the DSM-III allowing for multiple *Axis One Disorders*, thus legitimizing the notion of co-occurring disorders (Osher & Drake, 1996). It also became clear that sequential treatment of co-occurring disorders was not working very well. More often than not, persons with co-occurring disorders would be bounced back and forth between mental health and substance abuse systems that often followed conflicting treatment philosophies. Unfortunately, this problem frequently persists today (National Mental Health Association, 2002, p. 3). One of the FTC Child Welfare Services (CWS) workers observed in this regard the following:

> We couldn't get one of our clients into mental health counseling. She kept getting passed around to different agencies so we couldn't return her kids until she got the treatment.

In the 1990's the federal government recognized the existence of co-occurring disorders by creating the Substance Abuse and Mental Health Services Administration (SAMHSA). SAMHSA was authorized to oversee strategies for serving persons with co-occurring disorders (Osher & Drake, 1996). Although funding streams for the treatment of substance abuse and mental health remained separate, there was a growing awareness that persons with co-occurring disorders needed integrated services that treated both disorders simultaneously, not sequentially (National Mental Health Association, 2002, p. 3). In 1999, the National Association of State Mental Health Program Directors (NASMHPD) and the National Association of State Alcohol and Drug Abuse Directors (NASADAD) suggested language for the SAMHSA federal reauthorization statute that stated the following: "Block Grant funds could be used to fund services for persons with co-occurring disorders as long as the funds are used for the purposes for which they are authorized by law and can be appropriately tracked." This language marked the beginning of flexible funding for co-occurring disorders (National Mental Health Association, 2002, p. 3).

Although drug courts and mental health courts have been established to help address these issues, judges and treatment personnel remain frustrated in their attempts to meet the needs of individuals with co-occurring disorders as available treatment providers do not offer adequate services (National Mental Health Association, 2002, p. 6). A 2002 U.S. Department of Health and Human Services Studies report concluded that few providers or systems that treat mental illnesses or substance use disorders address the problem of co-occurring disorders adequately ("Report to Congress," 2002). This conclusion is still accurate. According to the 2009 National Survey of Substance Abuse Treatment Services, only 36% of the nation's treatment facilities offer special programs or support groups for clients with co-occurring mental health and substance abuse disorder (U.S. Department of Health and Human Services, 2009, p. 4). Only 30% of treatment facilities considered a mix of mental health and substance abuse treatment services to be their primary focus (p. 1). In Washington State, 32% of the four hundred thirty-four treatment providers indicated they had special programs for co-occurring clients (p. 4). Only 25% of substance abuse treatment providers reported having a mix of mental health and substance abuse treatment services as their primary focus (p. 1).

Serious Mental Illness (SMI) is defined officially as having a diagnosable mental, behavioral, or emotional disorder that met the criteria found in the 4th edition of the *Diagnostic and Statistical Manual of Mental Disorders* (DSM-IV) and resulted in functional impairment that substantially interfered with or limited one or more major life activities. Past research has determined that more than 19% of people with mood disorders, such as depression, also abuse drugs other than alcohol or nicotine. Among people whose primary disorder is drug abuse, mood disorders were found to be 4.7 times more prevalent compared with the general population (Regier, Farmer, Rae, Locke, Keith, Judd, et al., 1990. Also see Fabricius, Langa & Wilson (2008) reporting 57.1% of 419 clients had one or more co-occurring psychiatric disorder, along with a substance-related disorder.).

For FTC clients in this study, 42% reported that treatment for psychiatric or emotional problems was "extremely important" to them at program entry.[5] However, only 8% of clients reported they were receiving mental health services at program entry. Another 14% were assessed by the treatment intake counselor as "in need" of mental health services. Interestingly, only one of the eighty-six clients assessed during the two-year study period was assessed by the treatment provider as having a co-occurring disorder at program intake.

The majority of people with co-occurring disorders rely on the public health (Medicaid) system that includes both federal and state "match" funds. However, Medicaid typically provides little coverage for substance abuse treatment (National Mental Health Association, 2002, p. 7), and significant barriers remain as the majority of drug court clients do not meet the state funding criteria for a 'serious mental illness.' According to one of the assistant attorneys general who helped create this program:

> The biggest obstacles for FTC clients are the mental health treatment services. Half of FTC clients don't meet the criteria for major mental health issues; PTSD, anxiousness, depression don't get you on GAU (General Assistance Unemployable). You need to have schizophrenia or be bi-polar to get state mental health assistance.

Similarly, a substantial body of literature based on empirical research exists regarding the treatment of persons with serious mental illness and a co-occurring substance use disorder (Mueser, Noordsy, Drake, Fox, 2003.) However, the treatment models developed for this population may not be applicable to persons with a co-occurring affective or anxiety and substance use disorder because the research upon which it is based is specific to individuals with serious mental illness—most typically psychotic disorders.

This distinction is important, because a majority of persons with a dual diagnosis have a co-occurring affective or anxiety disorder, which is not considered a severe and persistent mental illness (Kandel, Huang, & Davies, 2001; also see Kessler, Nelson, McGonagle, Edlund, Frank, & Leaf, 1996). Furthermore, the widespread application of these

---

[5] Percentages reported in this chapter include the 86 clients who were assessed for treatment. Information on these aspects of the comparison group are presented in later chapters.

models to broader populations involves substantial effort and expense (Watkins, Hunter, Burnam, Pincus, & Nicholson, 2005). NIDA Director Dr. Nora Volkow asserts in this regard, "It is likely that the high prevalence of co-occurring drug abuse and depression partly reflects overlapping environmental, genetic, and neurobiological factors" (Volkow, 2004, p. 714). For example, environmental factors associated with both conditions include family disruption, poor parental monitoring, poverty, and stress. Estimates derived from epidemiologic studies indicate that at least 40% of the vulnerability for addiction is related to genetic factors, while for depression estimates range widely between 24% and 58% (Volkow, 2004; also see Markou, Kosten, Koob, 1998).[6] Brain imaging studies have demonstrated that the same brain regions and structures are involved in mediating symptoms of depression and drug abuse, and rodent studies suggest that early exposure to certain drugs can lead to neurobiological changes associated with depression (Volkow, 2004. See also Markou, Kosten, Koob, 1998).

Cruelly, when FTC clients are provided a psychological evaluation, Child Protective Services (CPS) allots funds for the court-ordered evaluation, but not for any recommended counseling that results from a mental health evaluation (See Washington RCW 26.12.170; RCW 26.44.195). Further, when the state removes the children from the parents' care, the parents are not eligible for any state medical coupons for recommended psychological services. The FTC treatment supervisor points out:

> To receive services under Title XIX (Medicaid) funding, clients must have a documented mental health issue **and** have a child in the home.

This is a considerable difficulty for someone who needs to get sober and address their mental health issues <u>before</u> CPS will return their children to them. Because most FTC clients do not retain their state medical assistance during the initial phases of the program, and most do not meet the state criteria for mental health assistance, one FTC Assistant Attorney General astutely concluded:

---

[6] Twenty-six percent of FTC clients reported a family history of mental illness.

> The publicly funded mental health system is not available to our clients.

Meth Family Services had one licensed mental health counselor on staff who facilitated brief therapy to FTC clients for immediate needs that arose during their course of treatment (e.g., relapse, death of a loved one) for a brief six- to eight-session intervention. When the state gambling addiction money that funded his position ran out the counselor retired, and the program did not fill that position. One FTC AAG noted,

> The mental health counselor for [the FTC treatment provider] can handle less severe mental health cases, but we need one good, intensive counseling person. When you're clean, you still have mental health issues to contend with. We get them clean, but don't help them with underlying mental health issues that contributed to their substance abuse.

Treatment for chronic mental health issues of FTC clients had to be referred out, and the client needed a funding source other than FTC to access it. For long-term therapy, the majority of FTC clients could privately contract with CPS, go to the Community Health Clinic, or go to another mental health provider, depending on their financial eligibility. The FTC team discussed many times the idea of the chemical dependency treatment provider branching out to include mental health services. The Meth Family Services Program Director notes in this regard:

> To be certified as a mental health counseling facility, we would have to contract with the Regional Services Network (RSN). It's very expensive and would require us to develop a whole new set of policies and procedures. Another treatment provider did it, and it was costly.

One of the FTC chemical dependency counselors explained:

> A big challenge for the FTC program is the mental health piece. Ideally, most clients would benefit from it. A lot of the

women in the program see the mental health counselor for previous abuse issues.

Further, the majority of FTC clients must pay for their own mental health prescriptions.[7] For clients who are able to secure mental health prescriptions, many do not take them consistently enough to work effectively. Some would begin to feel better on the drugs and decide they do not need to take them anymore, impeding any prolonged progress they may have made in recovery. Others did not like the way the prescribed drugs made them feel and decided to stop the protocol without ever trying to discuss alternatives with a mental health provider.

Shortsighted policies such as these can cause some clients to take extreme measures in order to receive the services they need. One FTC team member recalled the following:

> One client threatened suicide to get into the intensive mental health treatment she needed. The child still didn't get the services he/she needed.

Existing policies also require clients to relapse, instead of maintain their clean time, in order to receive state-funded substance abuse treatment. Clients who qualify for the state's substance abuse treatment service can only access it if they have used drugs in the last sixty to ninety days. As a consequence, if a client wants to opt out of the federally-funded FTC program to enter a state-funded treatment program, they cannot qualify for state treatment funding if they have been successful in the federally-funded program for the past two to three months. This policy is also detrimental to FTC graduates who may relapse, as medical coupons do not cover either substance abuse or mental health aftercare services.

The unwillingness of policymakers to address mental health adequately is also very costly. A study conducted in Washington State found medical costs of Medicaid-only clients who received outpatient mental health treatment declined \$144 per person per month in the first year after treatment, and \$176 per person per month in the second year

---

[7] The federal Access to Recovery (ATR) grant did help a few of the FTC clients with mental health prescription costs.

compared to the change in costs among clients with mental illness who received neither psychotropic medication nor outpatient treatment (Mancuso & Estee, 2003, p. 35).

Courts can direct individuals to services, but those services must exist, in adequate supply, be accessible to court referrals, and be integrated to an extent that allows them to address the multiple and disparate needs of individuals with varying combinations of mental illness, substance abuse, housing, and medical needs. This means, regardless of what model a court adopts for the imposition of coercion or therapeutic jurisprudence, it is likely to fail in the presence of a substantial disconnect between the court and the systems providing mental health and substance abuse treatment (Grudzinskas, et al., 2005, p. 287). The failure of treatment providers to recognize and adequately treat these client issues works to the detriment of clients in recovery, the effectiveness of service providers, and the confidence in the justice system in parents' ability to recover and care for their children. Until treatment providers, government departmental managers and legislators acknowledge the need to address co-occurring mental health and drug use issues, treatment programs will likely continue to have mediocre success rates.

Housing

Housing has been identified by most drug court programs as the most immediate and critical need presented by many participants (Cooper, 2004, p. 5). Some clients are homeless at program entry; many others live in situations in which family members or other housemates are using drugs, thereby making efforts at abstinence extremely difficult (if not impossible). Until and unless these parents can make clean and sober living arrangements, any chance of their becoming free of drugs is rather slim (p. 6). Fifteen percent of assessed FTC clients reported that their home environment was not conducive to recovery, and another 20% were assessed at program intake as being homeless or in an unstable living environment. Half of assessed FTC clients reported an immediate household member or family member with a drug problem, while 33% reported an immediate household member or family member with an alcohol problem. Further, most drug court participants lack the resources to find appropriate housing on the open market (p. 5). Forty-four percent of FTC clients were assessed at program intake as not having funds for basic needs.

Unfortunately, treatment programs are not very helpful in this regard. The FTC judge observed:

> Our housing piece stinks. People are on waiting lists forever. [Further] We have housing options for Moms with children, but nothing for Dads with kids."

One public defender stated:

> There's very little housing to choose from. Publicly-funded housing is a year out. If your child is to be returned in two months, that's a problem. Further, if you have a drug felony, you can't get into publicly-funded housing.

An FTC treatment counselor noted the following:

> We have housing resources, it's just hard. Clients come into this program and don't work for the first eighteen weeks [to concentrate on recovery, as suggested by the treatment provider.] It's hard to get clean and sober housing without a job.

To further complicate matters, housing is the last issue that a dependency addresses. One FTC treatment counselor stated:

> Clients can't get subsidized housing until CWS commits to returning their children within 30-45 days.

Once a housing voucher is issued, the recipient has ninety days to find housing that accepts those vouchers. However, even the eligibility for housing vouchers is not clear-cut. One housing voucher contractor who would provide vouchers to FTC clients if the only thing preventing parent/child reunification was housing, denied an FTC client a housing voucher because she was reunified with her child while living in transitional housing.

Public housing resources, including those made available under the Housing Opportunity Program Extension (HOPE) Act of 1996 (Public Law No. 104-120) would theoretically provide an excellent resource for the drug court program and participants in need of housing. The reality, however, is that current statutory provisions and widespread local policies result in public housing being unavailable to most drug court participants (Cooper, 2004, p. 6). The HOPE Act was deemed a tough anti-crime measure designed to make public housing safe for law-abiding residents. However, two provisions of the law have potential detrimental consequences for persons involved with drug use or users, regardless of these individuals' subsequent success in recovery. The first provision requires that the lessee of any public housing unit assume an affirmative responsibility for the law-abiding behavior of all members of the lessee's household and guests. The second provision permits public housing authorities to deny admission to or evict individuals who have engaged in criminal activity, especially drug-related criminal activity, on or off public housing premises, regardless of whether they were arrested or convicted for these activities. As subsequently discussed, social and familial relationships of drug-dependent parents in recovery frequently threaten the parent's ability to maintain forward progress and sobriety and sustain family unity.

While the overall purposes of these statutes and policies are meritorious, the problem is that they are applied across the board with few exceptions. Occasionally, one hears of a local public housing administrator who has waived the "one strike" eviction policy for a drug court participant through special agreement with the court. However, that is a rare exception and generally only lasts as long as that particular administrator is in office. Housing and Urban Development (HUD) officials have indicated the "one strike" eviction policy is not a federal requirement, but rather a policy which local public housing authorities are free to disregard (See "Focus Group"). The reality is that the policy prevails in almost all jurisdictions and was upheld by the U.S. Supreme Court in 2002 (*U.S Department of Housing and Urban Development v. Pearlie Rucker, et al.*).

Cooper (2004) reports that several drug court judges have discussed with her the feasibility of proposing the development of an earmark for drug court participants in local public housing units to provide the court with a ready resource for drug court participants needing housing. Apart from the proposed earmark, simply permitting drug court participants to apply for and/or remain in public housing units would seem to be a helpful policy change. The participant and/or his/her family would have a drug-free place to live, and the neighbors could have substantial confidence that the participant/resident was being tested for drugs frequently and closely supervised by the court (p. 7).

When the Project Vouchering for Drug & Family Court Participants Affordable Housing Trust Fund and Pilot Project began December 1, 2004 with the local Housing Authority in the jurisdiction studied here, ten slots were designated for drug court clients. This program filled a significant need for drug court clients. People in recovery who were clean and sober (must be in Phase II of FTC) could stay up to two years, and they did not need to have custody of their children in order to live there. The program required payment of 30% of each resident's income.[8] Relapses were tolerated, but being kicked out of your drug treatment program could result in the loss of the housing. When the Housing Authority voucher program began placing tenants, nine of the ten drug court slots went to felony drug court clients and only one went to family treatment court. While several housing assistance programs exist for FTC clients, their availability and efficacy in helping clients achieve permanent sober housing remains dubious.

Employment and Income

According to the National Low Income Housing Coalition's Out of Reach Report published in 2005, a person in the community studied here had to make at least $12.19 per hour ($1,950.40 per month for a 40-hour per week job) in order to rent a modest 2-bedroom house (Out of Reach, 2011).[9] In the FTC program, 74% of assessed clients were unemployed at program entry. Only 8% were employed full-time, and some of their employers would not allow them time off work to attend

---

[8] The 2000 census reported 39% of county residents paid more than 30% of their monthly income on rent.

[9] Washington State's minimum wage in 2005 was $7.35 per hour, according to the state Department of Labor and Industries.

their monthly or bimonthly court date. Forty-two percent of the clients were assessed at program entry as not having employment opportunities.

The self-reported average monthly income for assessed FTC clients for 2003 through 2005 was as follows:

Mean = $634.42
Median = $440 (TANF)
Mode = $0

Clients' monthly income ranged from $0 to $3,500.[10] The bottom 25% capped at $38.84 per month, and the 75% quartile started at $1,000 per month. Clients did everything from regularly give blood, to pawn their car title in order to have money for mere necessities. One treatment counselor noted:

> Many of our clients don't have extensive employment experience, so we devise a "self-employment" list (e.g., mowing lawns, babysitting) to come up with an employment history.

Another treatment counselor observed:

> There are jobs, but you have to swallow your pride and take a telemarketing or restaurant job. Clients who are motivated get a job.

FTC clients (especially fathers) had to be creative in keeping employment, especially during their participation in the most rigorous Phase I of the treatment program. Their creativity sometimes put them at risk for relapse:

> Staying up at night is going to get you. If you're up when all of your using friends are up, they come and see you, you run into them at the store. Peer pressure (to use drugs) at night is the worst.

---

[10] In verifying the high-end number with the team, they were highly skeptical of the accuracy of the $3,500 monthly income reported by the former client.

Relationships

Research has shown that the second most divisive and destructive influence in a family drug court is the continuing romantic relationships of participants with partners who continue to use drugs (McGee, et al., 2000, p. 50; also see Fals-Stewart, et al, 2000). Practitioners agree that to the extent possible, effort should be made to try to enroll significant others in the program itself and get them sober as well. Some of them, however, are violent and need to be the subject of protective orders. A partner may also be in jail or prison and seek to rebuild the romantic relationship upon their release. For the women in recovery, these are very powerful influences that cannot be ignored. Often a parent in treatment will start to think "straight" for several months only to again become 'less clear-headed' when a prior lover or spouse walks back into their already unstable lives.

A longitudinal analysis of the Glueck and Glueck (1950) data of males with a history of juvenile delinquency by Sampson and Laub found the following: "Strong attachment to a spouse (or cohabitant) combined with close emotional ties creates a social bond or interdependence between two individuals that, all else being equal, should lead to a reduction in deviant behavior" (Sampson & Laub, 1993, p. 140).

In the current study, an interesting twist on this finding emerged. First, the majority of FTC clients (over 70%) were women, and the majority of these women had a male partner with whom they used drugs – often the father of the child(ren) in the open dependency. Both were committed to staying together and to regaining custody of their children; and each served as the other's biggest relapse trigger. In this analysis, the "strong attachment to a spouse (or cohabitant) combined with close emotional ties [that] create a social bond or interdependence between two individuals" oftentimes served as a tormented push-pull between deviant and conventional behavior.

Simons, Stewart, Gordon, Conger & Elder (2002) stipulated that association with offenders is diminished only if one's romantic partner is committed to a conventional lifestyle. Living with a partner who engages in unlawful behavior actually enhances the probability of crime for men and women, and these romantic relationships appear to exert a greater negative influence on women. Conversely, Mears,

Ploeger, and Warr (1998) found that although both males and females are influenced by associations with criminals to engage in unlawful acts, females are less affected by these associations.

Hence, the issue of treating parenting couples in family treatment court is a complicated one. Frequently, the biggest hurdle to a client's family reunification and sobriety was sitting next to them in treatment court, sharing their dinner table, and possessed the exact same tentative level of parental rights they did. Both were mandated by the state to sober up or lose their family, but each had their own method, pace and struggle in doing their part to achieve that goal. Most of these clients experienced tumultuous relationships that hinged on drug use, and typically included poverty, a history of family violence, and feature an audience of children. Family treatment courts must therefore address issues such as:

- How to counsel clients whose partner may be their main relapse trigger, but with whom the client wants to stay together.
- What to do in terms of program participation and child
- reunification if one parent does well in the program, but the other does not.
- How to handle partners with a history of domestic violence
- (i.e., How to protect victims while simultaneously treating their abuser.)

In an effort to address these concerns, one of the treatment counselors who was certified for mental health counseling facilitated a couples group for client partners. The group focused on honest communication and the development of sober coping skills.

The issue of relationship showed CWS in a most omnipotent light. In FTC team meetings, the child welfare workers were often questioned by the team when they asserted that any person living in or visiting a client's home must be approved by the Department. The public defenders argued that CWS had no legal right to regulate client relationships. CWS would agree, then clarify that their function was child protection, and any drug-using adult threatened child safety – an issue well within their enforcement powers. The treatment counselors, and indeed all of the team members, frequently struggled with explaining these intricacies to the clients' satisfaction.

Transportation

Transportation is often another difficult issue for treatment court clients (Grella, 1999; Friedmann, Lemon, & Stein, 2001; Olmstead & Sindelar, 2004). Only 37% of assessed FTC clients possessed a valid driver's license at program entry; however, 44% reported having access to an automobile. CWS provided a monthly bus pass or gas stipend to assist clients with their transportation needs. For clients living further away, however, the bus system was very cumbersome, taking two hours to get from their home to the downtown treatment facility or treatment court. For clients who have their own transportation, it was often unreliable, causing them to be late to, or completely miss child visits, medical appointments, work days, or various treatment appointments – the latter of which resulted in a court sanction. Another problem with transportation is clients driving without a valid driver's license and/or auto insurance, particularly when they are transporting children who are in an active state dependency. To address this, the FTC treatment provider initiated a policy requiring clients to provide treatment counselors with these two items as an exercise in responsibility, to copy for their client file.

Childcare

Childcare is also a crucial issue for family treatment court clients (Grella, Polinsky, Hser, & Perry, 1999; Weisdorf, Parran, Graham, & Snyder, 1999; Olmstead & Sindelar, 2004). CWS cannot pay childcare for children not in a dependency [i.e., siblings of a dependent child]. To address this, the treatment provider occasionally used some of the treatment grant money to pay for childcare for children of FTC clients who were not part of the dependency. Once a client became employed, they were eligible for a different program that assisted with childcare expenses. One FTC graduate noted:

> WorkFirst paid for my oldest child's childcare because her father doesn't live with me, but they wouldn't pay for my

youngest child's care because his father and I live together with both children.

The client had to get a night job in order to make her household income exceed her childcare expenses.

Judge Charles McGee, who initiated the first family treatment court, asserts the following viewpoint concerning court responsibilities to clients in therapeutic court settings, "Unless the courts are willing to help create and monitor comprehensive services for families, then an excellent legal argument can be made that the state has violated its covenant to perform reasonable efforts to preserve and reunify the family within the tougher time lines set out in the [federal ASFA] Act" (McGee, et al., 2000, p. 24).

Pregnancy and Drug Use

The National Treatment Episode Data (2006) showed women comprised 31% of all treatment admissions; 4% of total treatment admissions were for pregnant women. The data also revealed that among women entering treatment in 2006, non-pregnant women were most likely to be admitted for alcohol use, followed by heroin and marijuana use. Pregnant women were most likely to be admitted to treatment with methamphetamine as their primary drug, followed by marijuana, PCP, or other stimulants (Substance Abuse and Mental Health Services Administration, 2008). Many studies of the effects of prenatal substance exposure compare methamphetamine-exposed infants to non-exposed infants without also comparing them to cocaine-exposed or other stimulant-exposed infants. As a consequence, it is not known whether the effects are associated with methamphetamine in particular or with all stimulants. The direct (when chemicals enter the fetus' blood system) and indirect effects (the decrease in blood flow to the fetus as a result of decreased blood from the mother) of substances, including legal drugs, tobacco and alcohol, can cause birth defects, fetal death, growth retardation, premature birth, dangerously low birth weight, and developmental disorders (Chasnoff, 1990). Methamphetamine and other stimulants jeopardize the development of the fetal brain and other organs (Shah, 2002). As was previously found with crack cocaine exposure, a high dose of methamphetamine taken during pregnancy can cause a rapid rise in temperature and blood pressure in the brain of the fetus, which can lead to stroke or brain hemorrhage. Prenatal stimulant exposure has been associated with difficulty in sucking and swallowing, and hypersensitivity to touch after birth (Anglin, Burke, Perrochet, Stamper, & Dawud-Noursi, 2000).

Drug-dependent mothers with high needs (or healthy) infants require comprehensive support. A compilation of studies show that the addicted pregnant woman is typically 27-31 years old, a high school dropout, has three or four children, and either lives in a drug-abusing environment or is homeless. She has been using illegal substances for at least ten years, and has grown up in a home with violence, sexual abuse, and substance-abusing relatives (Haack, 1997, p. 3). These demographics derived from other studies accurately describe the seven FTC clients (8%) who were pregnant at program entry. Of these, four were discharged and three graduated from the program. Pregnant women who applied to the FTC program or who struggled with sobriety while in the program were routinely referred to a local inpatient facility for pregnant and parenting women. The program was rigorous, however, and oftentimes only served to weed out clients who came in struggling with their recovery. The program did not allow clients to smoke, consume caffeine or sugar. When clients entered the six-month program, they began in the 'blackout' phase where no contact is allowed with friends, family, or significant others for several days. Each client was required to complete daily household chores, attend several group meetings per day, and exchange 'care fronts' with other household members. Care fronts are a self-governed accountability system designed to empower house members to watch over each other and identify any undesirable behaviors perceived to threaten the sanctity of the house or an individual's recovery. Former clients of the program report that, in practice, care fronts are little more than sanctioned gossiping and backstabbing exercises practiced by unhappy house members who lash out under the stress induced by the highly structured program.

While this program offers many of the necessary services for this specific population (e.g., safe, sober, transitional housing, on-site childcare and medical attention, individual and group counseling), the conditions of participation are often so demanding that the intended target population is, in effect, alienated from the treatment modality it needs most.

Fathers and Drug Dependence

Research that examines gender differences in drug and alcohol use, largely explore parenting only as an issue relevant to substance-abusing women. This emphasis on the ways the treatment needs of women differ from those of men has fostered the impression that parenting is not an important issue in the lives of substance-abusing men (McMahon & Rounsaville, 2002). Within the courts, too, there has been a focus on substance abuse as a legal issue relevant primarily in the lives of mothers (See: Oberman, 1992; Humphries, 1999; Jones, 1999; Paltrow, 1999 & 2010).[11] Consequently, there is relatively little information about fathering and father-child relationships occurring in the context of paternal substance abuse to inform decisions that must be made in family court (McMahon & Giannini, 2003, p. 342). Two studies published in 2007 that examined the characteristics of fathers with substance abuse issues found these men had similar backgrounds to mothers with substance abuse issues (i.e., typically: less than a high school education; wanted to parent their children, and, on average, had two children). Unlike mothers, however, fathers with drug issues were more likely to lose contact with their children as their relationship with their mother deteriorated, and were more likely to be a parental figure to children that were not biologically theirs. (McMahon, Winkel & Rounsaville, 2007 and McMahon Winkel, Suchman & Rounsaville 2007).

The limited information available regarding the parenting status of men with substance abuse problems makes it difficult to estimate accurately the number of alcohol or drug-abusing fathers present in the general population to fully inform family policy (McMahon & Giannini, 2003, p. 337). Secondary analysis by these authors of the 1994 National Household Survey on Drug Abuse data indicated that approximately 2.6 million (8%) of the 32 million fathers with minor, biological children had used an illicit drug during the past 30 days.

[11] See Kowalski (1998), noting that since 1985 at least 200 women have been prosecuted for substance use during their pregnancies.

Moreover, fathers with a recent history of illicit drug use were much more likely than fathers without a recent history of illicit drug use to be living away from all of their minor children (38.4% versus 20.7%, respectively). Fifty-nine percent of the fathers with a recent history of illicit drug use were living with at least some of their biological children.

When compared with men who have no history of alcohol or drug abuse, men with substance abuse problems are less likely to marry the mothers of their children, suggesting they are likely to appear in family court as unmarried fathers when there are questions about paternity, financial support, visitation, and custody (McMahon, 2002). Unfortunately, it is not presently clear how the compromise of father-child relationships in the context of chronic substance abuse affects child development (McMahon & Rounsaville, 2002).

One study comparing drug-abusing fathers to drug-abusing mothers did find that mothers who abuse drugs are more likely to allow their children to participate in interventions for substance abuse treatment than fathers who abuse drugs (Fals-Stewart, Fincham, & Kelley, 2004). The study involving 214 drug-abusing fathers and 106 drug-abusing mothers indicated that more than one-half of the mothers and only one-third of the fathers said they would consent to their children's participation in family or individual treatment programs. Factors associated with a mother's willingness to allow their children to receive help included higher reported levels of individual and family distress and social services referrals. However, the presence of a live-in partner was significantly associated with a mother's unwillingness to allow their children's participation in interventions because the action might anger the partner. For fathers, more frequent substance abuse in the year prior to program entry, family problems, referral by a legal agency, and increased psychiatric distress were all factors associated with reduced likelihood of allowing children's participation in family interventions. Fathers seemed more likely to characterize their problems as "personal" and needing to be addressed by them as individuals.

Preliminary research done with drug-abusing fathers indicates that guilt and shame about failure to fulfill social obligations as a father are prevalent in the lives of many substance-abusing men (Giannini, McMahon, Suchman, 2001; McMahon, 2001). Consequently, when dealing with substance-abusing men in family court, court personnel should be aware that guilt is typically associated with a desire to make retribution and repair interpersonal relationships, and although excessive feelings of guilt may be counterproductive, the guilt men do experience regarding their personal failures might be leveraged to promote beneficial change. However, court personnel should also be aware that shame is typically associated with a desire to actively avoid humiliating experiences, and it may be shame that causes men to deny their substance use, deny their family problems, and avoid family court proceedings. Although a common practice, shaming substance-abusing men in open court may only provoke negative feelings associated with similar experiences they have had as males in this culture and alienate them from a process that might otherwise prove helpful. Given traditional ideas about men and their obligation to provide financial support for their children, they may be particularly sensitive about their inability to provide financially for their family's needs (McMahon & Giannini, 2003, p. 344).

The FTC program affected this sensitivity by asking clients not to work during their first eighteen-week phase of treatment. One client stated:

> They told me to get a job, so I did. Then they told me I needed to quit so I could focus on my recovery.

Some jobs that fathers would take to work around their recovery schedule actually put them at risk of relapse:

> I had a seasonal job but had to quit because my co-workers used [drugs].

Further, if clients were able to get on the state's Division of Vocational Rehabilitation wait list [drug dependence is categorized as a Class 3 (lowest) disability], their wait could go on for more than two years before they are offered employment assistance services.

A gender-bias did exist against fathers in FTC. One example involved the CPS-supervised visitation rooms, that were only open during work days. Working parents (mostly fathers) could not access this service as easily due to scheduling conflicts. If their children were not in a relative placement where they could visit them during evenings or weekend, they had severely limited visitation opportunities. One child welfare worker observed the following:

> We have contracted providers for after hours and weekends, but they are very limited.

The FTC judge noted:

> Visitation should be some place that is a little less artificial in its surroundings (than the visitation rooms at DCFS). There should be more visitation options for parents.
>
> Further, while there are several local inpatient treatment facilities for mothers and children, no similar program exists for fathers. In addition, CWS did not allow fathers who were in an inpatient treatment facility to have visits with their children at the facility because of child safety concerns (i.e., a group of male addicts in various stages of recovery.) Fathers were required to meet their children off-site, at the convenience of the Department, after the father had put in enough treatment time to earn off-site privileges.

Client Self-Sabotage

McGee (2000) notes that most of the participants in the drug court, as well as the drug court team members, truly feel as though they are doing something special by achieving sobriety, but he cautions against putting clients up on a pedestal where they probably do not belong. Most drug court participants come from backgrounds where their self-esteem is poor and sometimes nonexistent, and they often program themselves to fail. Some actually appear to be sabotaging their own recovery because they do not feel they are worthy of succeeding. This phenomena is widely present and the juvenile and family drug court judge has to be on the lookout for it (p. 51).

The FTC program witnessed this dynamic many times; unfortunately, some clients would excel in the program for extended periods and then seemingly inexplicably violate their program requirements by committing major infractions. These clients were often chosen as "stars" to represent the program out in the community, but they were never able to achieve the same level of confidence in themselves that other clients and treatment team members so clearly identified in them. In one team meeting the FTC team discussed their collective regret at putting a program client on such a symbolic high pedestal, feeling this action on their part may have deterred the client from asking for help "before he/she crashed" after leaving the program.

Parents with such complex life issues require a network of support that, in addition to addressing substance abuse issues, provides timely, comprehensive, long-term resources that assist clients with life, family and healthcare management issues – all of which can trigger relapse if not resolved during recovery.

CHAPTER 6

Administrative Issues in Recovery

The Status of Treatment Providers

Having identified the crucial needs for parents in recovery, it is disheartening to discover a dearth of relevant services for this population. As illustrated below in comparing national and state data from 2009 (U.S. Department of Health and Human Services, 2009.), less than 10% of treatment providers offer childcare assistance; approximately one in three drug treatment programs provide transportation or employment assistance to clients; less than half of such programs offer housing assistance; and roughly half of these programs provide social services to their clientele.

Funding: Sources and Issues

The Substance Abuse Prevention and Treatment (SAPT) Block Grant provides a substantial amount of the public funding for drug and alcohol treatment nationwide (Jones, 2004, p. 5). Despite this important funding source, treatment remains scarce and difficult to obtain. According to the 2010 National Survey of Drug Use and Health (NSDUH), 6.4 million people aged 12 or older "needed but did not receive specialty treatment for illicit drug use" (p. 83). This access problem is caused in part by the fact that private and public insurance policies frequently do not cover the cost of drug and alcohol treatment and states have faced unprecedented financial pressures over the past few years, thus making substance abuse treatment funding even more scarce and increasing the importance of the SAPT Block Grant. The

Targeted Capacity Expansion programs operated under the Centers for Substance Abuse Treatment also help meet the evolving needs of communities in need of substance abuse treatment. These programs are targeted, gap-filling services tailored to address specific and emerging drug epidemics and/or underserved populations, such as pregnant and parenting women (Jones, 2004, p. 6).

Increasing Medicaid coverage would expand access to alcohol and drug treatment for low–income women and children and other eligible populations. Many low-income individuals, including all women on welfare and those in families involved in the child welfare system, are eligible for Medicaid. However, Medicaid coverage for alcohol and drug treatment services for these individuals and families is unnecessarily limited. Dr. Hendree Jones (2004) cites two specific ways in which Medicaid coverage for alcohol and drug treatment could be enhanced:

1. Making alcohol and drug treatment a required service under the Medicaid program.

Medicaid finances some drug and alcohol treatment subject to state limits on amount, duration (generally 90-day maximum), and scope (least restrictive environment – i.e., start with outpatient, if that fails, move to inpatient), but alcohol and drug treatment is not a required service under the program. Because it is an optional service, only about twenty-five states have opted to cover drug and alcohol treatment services under their Medicaid benefit. States providing treatment to Medicaid clients can receive reimbursement if the treatment is provided under a Medicaid service category that qualifies for federal matching funds. The advantage of making alcohol and drug treatment required under Medicaid is that it would help establish a more stable source of funding for treatment that is not discretionary and subject to the annual appropriations process. Such stability in funding would increase access to treatment for low-income individuals and families who presently rely on limited Substance Abuse Prevention and Treatment Block Grant and scarce discretionary funds to support much-needed treatment services (Jones, 2004, p. 7).

2. Lifting the "IMD exclusion."

One of the most serious roadblocks preventing low-income individuals from obtaining residential alcohol and drug treatment has been the "Institution for Mental Diseases (IMD) exclusion." The IMD exclusion is a statutory provision that prohibits Medicaid from paying for institutional treatment for individuals between the ages of 22 and 64, who are diagnosed with mental disorders and receiving treatment in programs with more than sixteen treatment beds. In order for the Center for Addiction and Pregnancy (CAP) to receive Medicaid reimbursement for its patients in residential care, it must keep its residential program at sixteen beds or fewer. Also, individuals who enter IMD's lose their Medicaid eligibility for all Medicaid reimbursable services, including prenatal and HIV care – costly services which can drain scarce treatment funding if a program chooses to run a residential program larger than sixteen beds and thereby passes up Medicaid funding, or if the program is located in one of the approximately twenty-five states that does not cover alcohol and drug treatment services under its Medicaid benefit. While Congress never explicitly defined mental diseases to include alcoholism and drug dependence, the former Health Care Financing Administration (HCFA) interpreted mental diseases to include addiction. The simplest way to change the IMD exclusion would be to amend the regulations by removing "substance abuse" from the definition of "mental diseases" (Jones, 2004, p. 7).

Medicaid is also not enough of a support for clients' other needs. In Washington State in 2005, a mother with one child who qualified for state assistance received $440/month in Temporary Assistance to Needy Families (TANF), plus food stamps. However, parents could not get or keep TANF and state-assisted medical coverage if their child was removed from the home by the state. In addition to loss of TANF and medical support, clients who opted-in to the FTC (federally-funded) program could have lost up to $339/month living stipend in ADATSA (state) funding.

The National Center on Addiction and Substance Abuse at Columbia University reviewed federal, state and local budgets from 2005 to measure the impact of substance abuse and addiction on their health, social service, criminal justice, education, mental health, developmentally disabled and other programs in sixteen distinct budget categories (National Center on Addiction, 2009). Three findings from their research are particularly striking:

- In 2005, the federal government spent $238.2 billion on substance abuse and addiction or 9.6 percent of the federal budget. If substance abuse and addiction were its own budget category, it would rank sixth in size—behind social security, national defense, income security, Medicare and other health programs (p. 2).
- State governments, spent 15.7 percent of their budgets ($135.8 billion) to deal with substance abuse and addiction. If substance abuse and addiction were its own budget category, it would rank second behind elementary and secondary education. States spend more on substance abuse and addiction than they spend on Medicaid, higher education, transportation or justice (p. 2).
- Federal and state governments spend some $54 billion a year shoveling up after the substance abuse effects on children. The largest share is spent on the burden of substance abuse to the education system – $34 billion; another $15 billion is spent for children who are victims of child abuse and neglect; nearly $4 billion is spent for substance-involved youth caught up in the state juvenile justice systems (p. 17).

Due to the excessive need of comprehensive, long-term, immediately accessible substance abuse treatment programs, the FTC treatment provider was fortunate to receive federal funding from a U.S. Department of Justice, Office of Community Oriented Policing Services grant which they used to implement a family treatment court. This funding stream allowed FTC to offer *immediate* access to an intensive outpatient program for anyone with a history of meth use whose children were involved in a dependency due to the parents' drug use.

However, entering into "free" treatment has built-in financial challenges for court clients. An FTC treatment counselor explains the problem:

> In the beginning, when clients come into the FTC program, they have generally lost their TANF and their state medical benefits, and all they have are food stamps. They need a part-time job to afford living expenses. Yet in Phase I of the program (minimum of 18 weeks) we tell them we don't want them to work, but instead focus on their sobriety.
>
> There are limited resources for the homeless unless they are religious affiliated. For clients who are reluctant to stay in a religious-sponsored shelter, we tell them that's their rent – sitting in the religious services. Both the women's and the men's shelters are very structured living environments.

This is a difficult domestic shift for most drug-dependent clients to make. One client described her own experiences as follows:

> It was kind of scary. The whole time we were homeless we knew we could always go there (a shelter). But once you're there, you're in a confined area with all these rules. Someone knocks on your door at 5:30-6:00 am – and homelessness starts to look pretty good. But after a couple of months, you're grateful for the structure.

In 2004, Washington State was one of fourteen states to receive a 3-year federal Access to Recover (ATR) grant (U.S. Department of Health, 2006a). The $22.8 million grant was managed by the Washington State Department of Social and Health Services, Division of Alcohol and Substance Abuse, and provided funding for aftercare and recovery support services that are typically critical to the effectiveness of treatment. The Washington State Access to Recovery initiative focused on providing vouchers for substance abuse clinical treatment and/or recovery support services to low-income individuals in crisis who were involved with child protective services, shelters and supported housing, free and low-income medical clinics, and community detoxification programs (U.S. Department of Health, 2006b).

To be eligible, clients must:

- Have experienced a problem with alcohol and/or drugs
- Be motivated and want to achieve recovery
- Agree to participate in a chemical dependency treatment program (when there was a recommendation that they receive that type of treatment)
- Be 18 years of age or older
- Be at or below the 80% median income level for the state of Washington. (A family of one earning $27,332 in 2005 was eligible.) (Brunner, 2006).

Several FTC clients were beneficiaries of the ATR grant, which assisted them with securing housing, filling prescriptions, obtaining medical, and mental health care not provided by other services. However, due to the relatively high income threshold associated with the program, the available funding was allocated quickly and the program is currently not taking any new clients.

Even with these seemingly generous provisions, program clients had to access comprehensive services from various agencies and funding sources in a piecemeal fashion in order to meet their needs and those of their children. Clients often needed to visit several service providers in order to stay in treatment compliance: parenting classes; out-of-home visitation with children; health care appointments; mental health appointments; pharmacy; chemical dependency treatment; housing assistance; and vocational training. None of these services were co-located, and many clients had to rely on public transportation to fulfill their required appointments and treatment sessions.

CHAPTER 7

Anatomy of a Family Treatment Court

The family treatment court under evaluation began operating in January 2003 through the collaboration of:

- A substance abuse treatment program
- The State Department of Social and Health Services
- Division of Children and Family Services (DCFS)
- The State Attorney General's Office
- The County Public Defender's Office
- The County Court Appointed Special Advocates (CASA)/Guardian ad litem (GALs)
- The County Juvenile/Family Court

The intended purpose of the program was to provide CPS-involved parents with substance abuse issues *immediate* access to free substance abuse treatment. This yearlong, intensive outpatient program was funded via a U.S. Department of Justice, Office of Community Oriented Policing Services grant.

This family treatment court team was comprised of:

- 4 chemical dependency/mental health counselors
- 2 public defenders
- 2 state assistant attorneys general
- 1 CASA/GAL supervisor
- 3 DSHS child welfare caseworkers

- 1 child welfare supervisor

When the family treatment court officially began in 2003 it was funded to serve sixty-three families per year. The team's goal was to build the program up to manage sixty-three families at a time. However, the program seldom maintained more than twenty-two families at a time due to limited applicant interest based largely on the length and rigor of the treatment program. This unanticipated development resulted in the FTC treatment provider downsizing from three treatment counselors to two in 2004.

It should be noted that other family treatment courts have experienced similar circumstances. Harrell & Goodman (1999, pp. 19, 24 & 30) reported that when the Manhattan Family Court began in 1998, it enrolled 56 clients. The Suffolk County Family Drug Treatment Court established that same year accepts 30 eligible parents per year. Since the inception of the Escambia County Family Treatment Court in 1996, it has admitted 30 clients to its program each year.

Client Selection

Potential clients were made aware of the family treatment court by assistant attorneys general, DCFS workers or public defenders during their shelter care hearings, or through chemical dependency treatment providers or health care providers with whom the parents might come in contact. All of these parties provided the eligible parents with contact information for the treatment facility. Clients who called the program for more information completed a brief telephone intake interview and, if they were deemed eligible, invited to make an appointment to attend program orientation. In order to be eligible for participation in the family treatment court, potential clients must:
Have had an open child dependency case with the State (less than 6 months old)

1. Agree to the dependency (parents could not contest it)
2. Have a history of methamphetamine use
3. Have their 18th birthday before graduating the program

During the program orientation, the treatment provider informed potential clients of the program requirements and the graduated sanctions structure in place for program noncompliance. The program, which lasted a minimum of one year, was divided into three phases. Each phase required random UA testing, participation in several weekly treatment group and self-help meetings, one-on-one sessions with an assigned chemical dependency counselor, and attendance in family treatment court. The program requirements became less demanding as clients moved through the program phases and became better able to work on parenting, employment, housing, and mental health issues as needed (See Figure 7.1 at the end of this chapter).

In addition to attending program orientation, potential clients were required to observe at least three family treatment court sessions and be assessed by a program treatment counselor before opting into the FTC program. The treatment providers recommended that clients take two to four weeks to learn about and observe the program to help them make an informed decision as to whether they wanted to participate in this yearlong, intensive outpatient program.

Once a potential client completed their court observations, program orientation, and assessment requirements[12], the drug court team would meet to evaluate the needs of the client and assess the program's ability to meet those needs. The team discussed the parents' treatment needs, mental health issues, history with CPS, current living conditions, and client relationships that may interfere with recovery and jeopardize child safety. If the team felt the client was amenable to this intensive outpatient program, the client's CPS file was transferred to one of the three FTC child welfare (CWS) workers. If the team

---

[12] Treatment counselors used a state Division of Alcohol and Substance Abuse (DASA) Alcohol and Drug Addiction Treatment and Support Act (ADATSA) assessment tool that screened for: acute intoxication/withdrawal potential, biomedical conditions/complications, emotional/behavioral conditions, treatment acceptance/resistance, relapse/continued use potential, and Recovery Environment. Because the family treatment court program was federally-funded, this client data was not allowed to be entered into the state DSHS/DASA TARGET data set. Consequently, the researcher created a data set for this program population including clients and comparison individuals from 2003 through 2005 for the purpose of conducting this program evaluation.

declined the parent's admittance into the program, the parent remained in the regular CPS system and would likely be required by the court to complete a 90-day outpatient program as a condition of family reunification.

Pre-Court Treatment Team Meetings

Once admitted into the program, clients were divided into two groups: Group A and Group B. Each group had their own AAG and public defender who attended treatment court on alternating weeks with their client group. The chemical dependency counselors and child welfare workers did not split their team members according to these groupings, so they attended court every week. The assigned team members met for one hour every week prior to court to discuss the status of clients expected to appear that day.

Discussions in these meetings were generated from the treatment counselors' reports that briefly described clients' treatment progress or regression for the preceding two-week to one-month period (depending on which phase of treatment the client was in). Discussions consisted of clients' sobriety (clean/dirty UAs); attendance at self-help meetings; efforts toward securing housing, employment, and family reunification; severing ties with friends and/or family who threaten clients' recovery; any program violations clients committed; appropriate sanctions for the violation; and, any incentives clients earned for exceptional treatment progress.

Directly after these meetings, and just prior to court, the public defenders notified any client who would be sanctioned that day of the team recommendations in order to prepare any defense the client may offer. In court, the chemical dependency counselor read their report on each client aloud for the benefit of other clients (the judge was given a copy prior to court), then the AAG announced the team's recommendations for the client to the court. The judge asked for comments from the child welfare worker, GAL supervisor, public defender, and client, prior to making a ruling from the bench. When the client's progress was satisfactory or excellent and no ruling was necessary, the judge used this time to briefly converse with the client to get a first-person account of the client's experiences during their participation in the program.

Graduated Sanction Agreement

When opting into the program, clients signed a two-page Treatment Agreement that included a list of the programs graduated sanctions:

- Verbal reprimand by the court
- Jury Box (clients were sent to Felony Drug Court to observe people who may be further along on their addiction path and more involved in the criminal justice system.)
- Held back from progressing to the next level (phase) of treatment
- More intensive treatment required (e.g., inpatient)
- More frequent UA/BAs
- Community Service
- Loss of unsupervised visits with children
- Up to 5 days in jail
- Termination from Family Treatment Court and returned to Dependency Court
- Child removed from parent's home to protect the safety of the child

Also listed in the Treatment Agreement are the three types of discharge from the program:

- *Successful Discharge*: Successful completion of all program requirements.
- *Neutral Discharge*: Client chooses to discontinue participation at any time and return to Dependency Court.
- *Unsuccessful Discharge*: Family Treatment Court notified Dependency Court of any unsuccessful discharges from the FTC program.

Clients could choose to opt out of the program at any time without penalty. They were, however, required to fulfill any pending sanctions before opting out of the program. The family drug court team did try to work with the client to help them remain in the program, but ultimately the decision was solely the client's. Clients could be discharged from the program for habitual non-compliance. For clients who opted out or were discharged from the program, their case was referred back to dependency court where they were assigned a different DCFS caseworker and public defender.

A flowchart of the drug treatment court process follows. Recall that the study population were CPS-identified parents with an open dependency case due to substance abuse issues. Eighty percent of potential clients were referred from shelter care hearings by AGs, PDs, or CPS; 20% of potential clients were referred by other treatment providers, friends, family or were self-referred.

Figure 7.1: Family Treatment Court Client Flowchart

Orientation

The treatment provider informs potential clients about the requirements of the program:

- Minimum 12-month, intensive outpatient treatment.
- 3 treatment phases, with each progressing from more program accountability towards more personal accountability.
- Graduated sanction schedule.

Treatment Assessment

The treatment provider assesses the treatment needs of clients still interested in participating in the program.

Figure 7.1 (Continued): Family Treatment Court Client Flowchart

Family Treatment Court Team Review

FTC team members (AGs, CPS, PDs, GAL, CD Treatment Providers) review the case and discuss the potential fit between the program services and the individual's needs.

Treatment Planning

Could include:

- Parenting Classes
- Anger Management Training
- Domestic Violence Perpetrator Treatment
- Mental Health Counseling
- Vocational Rehabilitation
- GED Program

Implementation

Clients approved by the treatment team enter the program and progress at their own pace through the three phases of treatment.

Figure 7.1 (Continued): Family Treatment Court Client Flowchart

Phase I – 18 weeks minimum

Each phase includes:

- Treatment group sessions
- Random UAs
- 1:1 counseling sessions
- Verified self-help group attendance
- Family treatment court attendance

Clients may begin to address any medical/dental issues.

Phase II – 18 weeks minimum

- Clients proceed with less frequent, random UAs & group attendance.
- Clients begin any specialized groups recommended in their Treatment Plan.
- Clients may begin to seek employment.
- Clients may be granted more, longer, or unsupervised visitation with children.
- Clients may secure an income source (TANF, employment).

Figure 7.1 (Continued): Family Treatment Court Client Flowchart

Phase III – 16 weeks minimum

- Clients proceed with less frequent, random UAs & group attendance.
- Clients begin to secure housing for the return of their children.
- Clients may be granted more, longer, or unsupervised visits with children.
- Clients secure an income source (TANF, employment).
- Clients graduate from program

CHAPTER 8

Client Characteristics

Life course theory pioneers Thomas and Znaniecki (1918) asserted:

> A social institution can be fully understood only if we do not limit ourselves to the abstract study of its formal organization, but analyze the way in which it appears in the personal experience of various members of the group and follow the influence which it has upon their lives. There is no safer and more efficient way of finding among the innumerable antecedents of a social happening the real causes of this happening than to analyze the past of the individuals through whose agency this happening occurred (Vol. 3, p. 7).

It is through this epistemology that this family treatment court was evaluated. The research data collected for analysis consisted of:

1. Review of treatment intake assessments
2. Review of treatment progress reports
3. Review of portions of client and comparison group DSHS files
4. Client post-program interviews
5. Client post-program survey data
6. Recorded weekly courtroom observations for two years
7. Recorded weekly treatment court team meeting observations for two years
8. Interviews with treatment court team members

The triangulation of data sources was used to enhance data integrity and provide an accurate picture of the outcomes experienced by both FTC clients and the comparison groups associated with the FTC evaluation study.

The Family Treatment Court Client Characteristics

Tables 8.1 and 8.2 provide demographic comparisons between the family treatment court and the surrounding county. The FTC data set for this research was comprised of 124 individuals who called the treatment provider and expressed an interest in the program between January 1, 2003 and December 31, 2005. The 124 individuals were divided into three distinct groups:

- Graduates (44) – individuals who successfully completed the program.
- Early Outs (44) – individuals who left the program prematurely, either by being discharged or voluntarily opting out.
- Comparison Group (36) – individuals who called to inquire about the program but chose not to participate

The statistics set forth in Table 8.2 indicate that the FTC program population is similar in racial composition to its surrounding community. However, the FTC group is quite clearly much less educated and is seeking to manage a family unit with far fewer economic resources than is the case for the broader community.

Tables 8.3 and 8.4 provide a variety of descriptive statistics of the eighty-six people assessed for the FTC program between the dates January 1, 2003 and December 31, 2005 at program intake. Tables 8.3 and 8.4 do not include thirty-eight people who were part of this research study, but were not assessed by the FTC program.[13]

[13] Two individuals who entered the FTC program were assessed by another agency. The assessment tools used for these individuals were dissimilar and incomplete so they are not included in this section.

Table 8.1: Program and County Racial/Ethnic Comparison

Race/Ethnicity Comparison: FTC vs. County Population	FTC Data Set (1/1/03-12/31/05)	County* (2004)
Caucasian	88%	92%
Native American	8%	1%
African American	3%	2%
Native Hawaiian/ Pacific Islander	1%	1%
Asian	---	2%
Multi-racial	---	2%
Latino Ethnicity (can be any/no race listed above)	2%	3%

* Figures based on U.S. Census Bureau and Office of Financial Management demographic estimates for the county.

Table 8.2: Program and County Education, Employment & Income Level Comparison

	FTC Data Set (1/1/03-12/31/05)	County (2004)
No high school education	41%	11%^
Unemployed	70%	6.5%^
Lived Below 200% of the Federal Poverty Level	90%ˇ	33.2%*
Lived Below 100% of the Federal Poverty Level	73%ˇ	16.7%*

^ According to the County Health District Poverty and Health Indicators, 2005 Update.

ˇ The 2004 FPL was $12,490 for two people ($9,310 for 1 person). The above percentages were based on client reported monthly income and marital status.

*According to the State Employment Security Department, Labor Market Economic Analysis Branch.

Table 8.3: Education, Employment & Income Data for FTC Clients

Education	
High School Diploma/GED	45%
No Academic Degree/No Education	40%
Vocational Training/AA Degree	13%
Missing Data	2%
Employment	
Unemployed, Not Seeking Work	42%
Unemployed, Seeking Work	30%
Employed (Full-time, part-time, temporarily)	15%
Homemakers	7%
Disabled	4%
Missing Data	2%
Primary Source of Income	
No Primary Source of Income	34%
Public Assistance/SSI/SSDI/Disability	32%
Other/Friend/Family	19%
Work/Salary	13%
Missing Data	2%

Table 8.4: Client History of Abuse

FTC Clients Reporting:	Assessed Clients*	% Female
Family History of Substance Abuse	77% (59/77)	76%
Personal History of Emotional Abuse	82% (64/78)	81%
Personal History of Physical Abuse	68% (53/78)	81%
Personal History of Domestic Violence Abuse	62% (51/82)	86%
Personal History of Sexual Abuse	53% (41/77)	88%

*This table depicts data from the program intake forms and therefore does not include members of the control group. The Assessed Client percentages represent the number of affirmative answers as relative to the number of total subjects (out of 86) for which data was provided on the given variable.

Clients self-reported a total of 54 arrests in the year prior to program entry. They also reported being charged in 173 events, with a total of 382 criminal charges associated with those events ranging from vehicular homicide to a variety of property crimes over their lifetime.

Physical and Psychological Conditions of Study Subjects

Twenty-six percent of FTC clients reported a current physical illness that needed to be addressed or that would complicate treatment. As depicted in Table 8.5, over half of FTC clients felt some level of need for treatment of psychiatric or emotional problems that might interfere with their substance abuse treatment.

Table 8.5: FTC Clients Who Perceived an Immediate Treatment Need for Psychiatric/Emotional Problems at Program Intake[14]

Extremely	41%
None	41%
Considerably	7%
Moderately	5%
Slightly	4%
Data Missing	2%

Table 8.6: FTC Clients with Psychiatric Evaluation at Program Entry

No Current Psychiatric Evaluation	64%
Problem Diagnosed with Previous Evaluation	17%
Psychiatric Evaluation Made, No Problem Found	8%
Assessed as Needing Re-evaluation	6%
Problem Indicated and Referred for Services	5%

[14] Mental health symptoms listed on the intake assessment form were: anxiousness/nervousness; sleep disturbances; phobias/paranoia/delusions; eating disorders; hallucinations; serious depression; hostility/violence; referral to mental health; grief and loss issues; inability to comprehend and; loss of appetite.

Table 8.7: FTC Clients Reporting Receiving Mental Health or Psychiatric Help

Previous Mental Health Care	
Ever Received Mental Health Counseling or Psychiatric Help	42%
Received Mental Health Treatment in the Past Year*	23%
Current Mental Health Care	
Taking Medications for Mental Health Purposes	20%
Taking Psychiatric Prescriptions	16%
Parent Receiving Mental Health Services	7%
Needing Mental Health Care	
Assessed as "In Need" of Mental Health Services	13%

*80% of clients who received mental health treatment in the past year did so in conjunction with outpatient treatment; 20% received mental health treatment with hospitalization.

Table 8.8: FTC Clients Reporting Suicide Symptoms at Program Intake*

1 Suicide Symptoms	45%
2 Suicide Symptoms	35%
3 Suicide Symptoms	26%
4 Suicide Symptoms	13%

*Suicide symptoms listed on the intake assessment were: Hopelessness; decreased energy; giving away valued possessions; moodiness; preoccupied with death; sleeplessness; withdrawn; self-destructive, and takes unnecessary risks. It is important to note that many of these can also be attributed strictly to clients' children being removed from the home and/or the abrupt change in drug use.

The national suicide rate is approximately 11/100,000 (.011%) (U.S. Department of Health, 2009, p. 5). While there are no national data on attempted suicide in the U.S., estimates vary between 88/100,000 (.088%) and 250/100,000 (.25%) (National Institute of Mental Health, 2001; American Association of Suicidology, 2003). Notably, 23% of FTC clients reported attempting suicide at some time in their lives, and 5% reported having a family history of suicide.

Based on these data, the typical family treatment court client in this study was Caucasian, had no more than a high school education, was unemployed, had an extensive history of emotional, physical and/or sexual abuse, was in need of mental health care, and more likely than the general population to experience suicidal tendencies.

Study Population Demographics

The following table provides demographic comparisons of 44 graduates, 44 "early out" individuals who were either discharged from the program (28) or who opted out (16) of the FTC program, and 36 "comparison" individuals who called the FTC treatment provider to learn more about the program, but who chose not to opt-in to the program.

The following chapters discuss the program characteristics, program outcomes, and program issues that arose for this client population.

Table 8.9: Parent Demographics

	Graduates (44)	**Early Outs** (44)	**Comparison** (36)
Race			
Caucasian	95%	77%	92%
Native American	5%	12%	8%
African American	---	9%	---
Pacific Islander	---	2%	---
Ethnicity			
Latino	4%	9%	---
Gender			
Female	70%	79%	84%
Male	30%	21%	16%
Age Group			
20-25	14%	23%	28%
26-30	16%	31%	25%
31-35	35%	30%	36%
36+	36%	16%	11%

These selected demographic comparisons indicate that the FTC graduate group tended to have a greater proportion of older (over 30) members than either the early out or comparison group. These comparisons also indicate that program graduates consisted of a higher rate of male members than either the early out or comparison group, and that they had a considerably higher percentage of Caucasian members than did the 'early out' group.

CHAPTER 9

Family Treatment Court Program Characteristics

An important component of this research involves a process evaluation of the FTC program. Two years of recorded observations in weekly treatment team meetings, individual team member interviews, post-program client interviews and surveys provide an in-depth examination of how the program was set up to work, how it works in practice, and how it has evolved over the two-year study period. Through client treatment progress reports, FTC client experiences were reviewed and compared to determine whether clients were treated equitably by the family treatment court team regarding compliance with program requirements, service referrals, receipt of incentives, and the imposition of sanctions. This process evaluation also includes an assessment of the program's ability to match client service needs with relevant and accessible services, both within the program and through referrals to other service providers to identify any gaps in the current provider system. Client needs commonly included:

- Referral to an inpatient program when failing to maintain sobriety through FTC.
- Medical services when state assistance was discontinued due to state removal of children.

  Prescriptions and medical assistance for psychotropic medications and/or mental health counseling for clients with co-occurring disorders.

- Safe, affordable, sober, temporary housing that was ready when clients' children were returned home
- Safe, affordable childcare
- Employment/Income
- Professional Development/Higher Education

The Treatment Team: Workgroup Characteristics

This research also examined the workgroup dynamics of the family treatment court team, discussing the capacity of team members to work together to reach consensus on clients while remaining dutiful representatives of their respective agency and/or client, and the willingness and ability of the treatment team to problem-solve and make adjustments as client needs arise (See Eisenstein & Jacob, 1991: Ch. 2 & 3; McCoy, 2003; Etienne, 2003; Trujillo, 2004). It is a complex undertaking for treatment team members from such diverse organizational cultures to hone a communication style that is both understood and accepted by all other team members.

The following roles filled by team members heavily influenced the workgroup dynamics in the family treatment court:

- The judge served as the team leader and client mentor in family treatment court. The FTC judge also presided over dependency court for FTC, and non-FTC families.[15]
- CWS personnel advocated for the best interest of the children in the dependency.[16] CWS caseworkers attended both family treatment and dependency court hearings.
- The assistant attorneys general represented CPS in both the family treatment court and dependency court.
- Public defenders represented the parents in both family treatment and dependency court.

---

[15] In addition to a bi-monthly review in family treatment court, FTC clients attend dependency court reviews every three months.

[16] CPS is the only FTC agency governed by a federal timeline. According to ASFA guidelines, they must have a permanency plan in place for dependent children within 14 months of removal from the home.

- Drug treatment counselors were advocates for the parents' sobriety. They attended family treatment court, but not dependency court.
- Guardians ad litem were the "child's voice" in court. They attended dependency hearings, but only their supervisor attended family treatment court and the FTC team meetings.

With the exception of the judge who served a two-year term for the FTC, other team members could remain on the team indefinitely.

Because individual team member foci are essentially split between parent and child, it was vital that all team members communicated their respective concerns clearly for consideration by the rest of the team. One treatment counselor explained the dynamics of this communication thusly:

> Treatment counselors and CWS workers felt like opposing teams, so we meet to educate each other. We did not expect that in the beginning, but we serve essentially two different clients so it makes sense that it feels that way.

Further, because each of the team members has a unique focal point, a delicate balance must be maintained when exchanging information between treatment providers, CPS, and the courts. Parents have a right to be protected from having all information divulged in their individual and group treatment sessions forwarded to the treatment team by their counselor. At the same time, the protection of the child requires that parents be held accountable for meeting standards laid out in court orders through information gathered by their CPS worker and guardian ad litem (Harrell & Goodman, 1999, p. 32). One treatment counselor explained the situation as follows:

> Clients view CPS as the enemy and treatment as the ally. Treatment feels that clients are more forthcoming with information with them than with CPS.

While clients were held accountable for their drug use through UA results that were shared with the team, treatment counselors felt that clients should be able to freely express both positive and negative feelings and thoughts about drugs in treatment sessions during the recovery process without fearing program repercussions.

Harrell & Goodman (1999) note that each agency must respect the professional knowledge and experience of the others. In practice, treatment providers should have the last word in clinical decisions, and CWS and child law guardians should have the last word on family reunification recommendations because their focus on the interests of the child must supersede the interests of the parent in treatment in these cases (p. 34). At times in the FTC team meetings, these decision lines became blurred. For example, CWS would condition the return of a client's children upon the parent's attendance at counseling sessions for abuse the parent experienced as a child, stating that these unresolved issues threatened the safety of the child in the current dependency. Treatment counselors countered that the client expressed an unwillingness to dredge up the old, uncomfortable feelings associated with such counseling, and that the client was doing well in his/her recovery. The AAG would side with CWS, and the public defender would usually defer to the wishes of the client, leaving the child advocate (GAL) supervisor with the deciding vote for the team's recommendation to the judge. If the team could not reach consensus on a course of action, the AAG informed the judge in court that the team did not have a recommendation for the client in question, and the judge would hear from all team members individually before rendering a decision. This was a rare scenario, however, as team members were skilled at listening to differing views and weighing which option would best accomplish client treatment goals and safe family reunification.

In a publication on family drug courts prepared for the Urban Institute, Harrell & Goodman (1999) assert that as discussions among agencies become more collaborative and open, policies and procedures for balancing these interests must be clearly identified and rigorously adhered to (p. 32). The FTC team members addressed this specific issue in two ways. First, they established monthly process meetings to discuss any program issues that arose. The judge attended these monthly meetings and served as facilitator and team leader to help the team work through any programmatic or administrative problems they identified. These scheduled monthly process meetings allowed the team to address divisive issues in a timely manner, before manageable disagreements developed into a full-scale breakdown in team communication that could negatively affect the program and the clients.

Approximately six months into the evaluation period, team members devised a second way to facilitate open communication and teamwork by instituting the three-way meeting with clients. As each new client entered the program, their treatment counselor and CWS worker scheduled a joint meeting with them. At that meeting, they reviewed the *Order of Dependency* that specified the court requirements for parents to regain custody of their children, and the client's *Individual Service and Safety Plan* (ISSP), written by the CWS worker to achieve the requirements listed in the court Order of Dependency. Each party received a copy of the two documents at the meeting, and questions or concerns were addressed immediately. The CWS workers and treatment counselors found that this process greatly improved their working relationship and enhanced their ability to guide their clients with confidence and clarity through treatment. The improved relationship also contributed to increased contacts between individual treatment counselors and CWS workers to clarify or problem-solve any client issues as they arose. The following section discusses in more detail, each team member's role in the program.

The Judge

Drug treatment courts require a shift in judicial role. Before the advent of treatment–based drug courts, the role of judges was to order addicts into treatment as a condition of return of the children, and judges were essentially not involved in supervising or monitoring the course of treatment. In many ways, it is a more natural transition for dependency/family court judges to incorporate the therapeutic philosophies embodied in treatment courts than for judges with criminal or other civil dockets. The best interests of the children require that family court judges examine the actual fitness of parents in custody, visitation, guardianship, and neglect/dependency/adoption cases, notwithstanding the substance abuse problems of the parent (McGee, et al., 2000, p. 6). The family drug court judge, therefore, needs to assess an additional level of complexity presented when one or both parents' substance use becomes an issue in these proceedings, as chemical dependency does not *per se* constitute parental unfitness.

Family drug court pioneer Judge Charles McGee (2000) notes:

> While sanctions for adult participants may involve temporary limits or restrictions on custody or visitation, such sanctions must first meet a threshold determination that the best interests of the affected children are being served. Existing custody or visitation will often still be appropriate notwithstanding a parent's dirty urine, a "slip", or minor relapse, but the court must still devise other effective sanctions to discourage drug use (p.7).

As a result of the planning and collaboration taking place between the various players in a family drug court program, and the central coordination and oversight authority of the judge, the drug court approach enables the judge to create system accountability where there usually is none. In turn, families are accountable in a system that previously has usually been unaccountable to them as well (McGee et al., 2000, p. 10; See also Eisenstein & Jacob, 1991, p. 21).

Based on data collected from focus groups of two pioneering family drug courts, drug court clients appear to view drug courts as essential resources in reshaping their lives.[17] Clients focus on the fact that a judge is at the center of the process and in control of the program. Clients fear jail, fear losing custody of their children, and fear losing their jobs. In fact, remarkably, they dread walking into the courtroom and being reprimanded by the judge in front of their peers (Goldkamp, White, & Robinson, 2000).

A key feature of treatment courts is that the judge meets regularly with each participant in open court to review their compliance or noncompliance with the conditions of his or her treatment. The purpose of these "status hearings" is to hold the participant publicly accountable through rewards in the case of successes, and graduated sanctions in the case of failures to adhere to the mandated therapeutic program (Boldt, 2002, p. 124). One FTC graduate stated:

> I only had one sanction – I was scared watching the others go to jail.

---

[17] Clark County, Nevada, and Multnomah County, Oregon.

Another graduate similarly recalled:

> I remember watching others get sanctioned and losing their kids. It was a reality check for me. It kept me in check.

The fact that drug court judges are directly involved in the various tasks of monitoring clients' behavior and imposing sanctions or conferring rewards is more than just for appearance sake. The judge's role in sanctioning and rewarding clients is to help them understand that their personal, private choices have consequences for which they will be held responsible, and that they control their own fate. Thus, when the judge responds promptly to a positive urine test or a missed group with a proportional sanction, he or she is helping to provide re-directive treatment to the client (Boldt, 2002, p. 124).

Critics of treatment courts assert that the formation of a direct relationship between judge and client has two significant, negative consequences. First, the "informality and immediacy of the judge's relationship with the treatment client confers a potentially ungovernable discretion" (Boldt, 2002, p. 125.) Critics note troubling similarities between drug courts and indeterminate sentencing schemes that were replaced by fixed sentencing structures to limit judicial discretion. Kittrie (1971) noted that under the auspices of rehabilitation, unfettered judicial discretion early on led to involuntary sterilization, lobotomy, and indeterminate incarceration. Further, critics assert that the direct relationship between the treatment court judge and the individual participant may tend to complicate the participant's relationship with his or her own attorney. The concept of counsel as an intermediary between the lay client and the court is likely difficult if not impossible to maintain in a drug court setting (Boldt, 2002, p. 125).

This dynamic of direct access and freedom of expression between clients and the judge occurred frequently in the FTC court. For example, early on in the program, after extremely abbreviated periods of sobriety some clients would appeal directly to the judge to increase their child visitation rights. The judge would look to the CWS worker in court for endorsement of an immediate proposed change in visitation. The judge would also ask the GAL program supervisor for informed input on the client's request. Because only the GAL supervisor and not the (largely volunteer) GALs attend FTC sessions, the supervisor would need to request a recess, attempt to locate the appropriate GAL by phone, and then advise the CWS worker so that a recommendation could be made to the judge. One CASA supervisor observed:

> In the beginning of FTC when clients wanted to increase visitation, they requested it in court. GALs need information from service providers besides treatment (e.g., parenting, appropriate housing) in order to make a determination on changes to child visitation.

One CWS worker noted:

> In the beginning, the judge would look to the CWS worker in court for an immediate [client requested] change in visitation. Now she asks the clients if they have talked to their CWS worker. Nine times out of ten, they haven't.

The team addressed this issue at one of their monthly process meetings, formally changing client visitation request procedures by requiring clients to address visitation questions directly to CWS. Clients could and did appeal to the judge regarding any real or perceived unsatisfactory progress by team members. In practice, the existence of a direct relationship between the judge and clients served to empower clients in a productive way rather than hindering their relationship with their public defender. The direct line of communication allowed clients to have a voice in their treatment progress instead of being a passive observer in a court while their lives were discussed at great length by everyone else in the room.

McGee (2000) notes, "The judge and the drug court staff must be able to perceive the depressions and frustrations that accompany an offender's struggle for sobriety. There will be ups and downs in every conversation with the offender. It is a mistake to encourage the participant to express a false level of enthusiasm. Let each court appearance reflect the energy and feelings of that moment" (p. 35). This approach was evident in the FTC program. The judge encouraged clients to speak in court. If clients prepared a written statement for the court either on their own, or to fulfill a sanction requirement by the treatment team, they were encouraged by the court to read it aloud. The catharsis this outlet provided to clients who were frustrated by the program or their progress was evident as they were provided an opportunity to speak freely, and address the court directly. It also provided clients an opportunity to shine and receive positive feedback from both their peers and the treatment team members for a carefully prepared, yet candid presentation.

McGee asserts that because of many clients' limited capability, the family treatment court judge must focus on short-term goals and avoid temptations to focus on long term challenges. He states, "Building a safe and secure future may be the best "reason" to enter the drug court treatment program. However, the necessity for prolonged achievement is often quite intimidating for an offender and hence may actually be a source of failure. The judge should ask participants about the issues they are dealing with on a daily basis and try to define the challenges they need to meet in their own terms" (p. 35). The FTC judge did this in a seemingly effortless way, asking clients about the here-and-now, and reminding clients of the long-term only in extreme cases of consistent program violation that appeared to be jeopardizing clients' prospects of reunification with their children.

Instead of being an instrument for judges to exercise unfettered discretion, family treatment courts appear to be a beneficial partnership between the government and local agencies' whose staff pool their limited resources to offer supportive services to parents seeking recovery, and to improve their abilities to meet the best interest of their children. It is a program of finite length, where clients are free to leave without jeopardizing their parental status (chronic relapse or other behaviors that put their children at risk may accomplish this, however), and clients are provided support for a prolonged period while they work on achieving their sobriety and attaining family reunification. Significantly, families involved in family treatment court would be under CPS supervision and required to remain sober and engage in services whether they chose either the traditional dependency system or the family treatment court program.

Criticisms of a lack of zealous advocacy or a resolute adversarial role by public defenders in a drug court setting lose much of their applicability when drug court is compared to plea bargaining – the most frequently used course of action in the justice system. The accused takes responsibility for specified harmful actions and agrees to complete various restorative activities as outlined by the state and reviewed by the defense. In addition, because the majority of family drug treatment courts are voluntary admits, the "punishment" is discharge from the program and redirection to another, often more abbreviated treatment program. As with a plea bargain, the client is provided the conditions prior to entering the program, and the consequences for not meeting the specified conditions. While persistent program violations can result in jail time for clients, the sanction is brief (less than one week), and the client can opt out once the sanction is satisfied. Further, it is likely that the client who remains on the path that lead him or her to a jail sanction in the program will meet with subsequent arrests for this same behavior outside the confines of the program, and will not have the supportive services to rely upon once they are released from custody.

Critics of the treatment court system also cite the dangers of drug court judges "wearing two hats" in the process: One as a neutral trier of fact; the other as the engaged, "hands-on" agent of therapeutic change (Terry, 1999, pp. 7-8). This position is much less compelling in light of decades (and the resultant *generations* of drug-involved people) of traditional court approaches that failed to address the myriad of individual and family problems stemming from substance abuse. This colossal failure lead to the justice system's recent focus on therapeutic jurisprudence and "problem solving courts" (e.g., drug courts, mental health courts, domestic violence courts, and the current "one family-one judge" philosophy of unified family courts.) Such courts require a shift in judicial philosophy where family treatment court judges remain the neutral trier of fact, but take a more direct role in seeking information from sources more varied than prosecution and defense counsel, including multiple service providers and the clients themselves. Further, because family treatment courts depend on the collaboration of several independent agencies to oversee these clients, each of whom has a specific focus, the prospect of unfettered, punitive and misdirected judicial discretion is rather unlikely.

To the contrary, the FTC judge was very cognizant and respectful of the rights of the program clients. She viewed weekly team meetings as *ex parte* communications, asserting that because the clients are not in attendance, and much of what the team discusses is not for the record, it was inappropriate for her to attend these pre-court meetings. Other FTC judges prefer to participate in the pre-hearing administrative meetings, concluding that by having representatives from all participants in the FTC proceedings present at these meetings, there is no ethical issue regarding *ex parte* communications (Edwards & Ray, 2005, p. 9).

The FTC judge's decision not to attend team meetings may have bolstered her ability to connect with clients directly, without relying on team members to serve as liaison. The judge did attend the monthly team process meetings, providing leadership to the treatment team and often acting as umpire to differing views by team members relating to program procedures (e.g., hair-splitting over what qualifies as a sanctionable event: What number on a BA machine qualifies as a "use" and therefore, noncompliance with the program?)

The observation period for this research covered the entire two-year rotation of this judge in FTC. She was the second judge to preside over the program, and the original FTC judge returned to the post at the conclusion of this judge's term. The FTC judge was well-matched to her family treatment court assignment. Her innate ability to lead from the bench through compassion, patience, and genuine interest in program clients, coupled with her clear expectation of full client accountability and candor, as well as team member answerability, proved very effective in guiding team members and clients through the program's progression. Representative comments from clients and treatment team members assessing the judge follow:

Client comments included:

> She [FTC judge] is wonderful. The most compassionate woman I've ever met.
>
> I loved her. She was so awesome. Judge [] even cares about the girls who aren't following the program. She's direct and to the point. Even when she had to send people to jail, you could tell she did it with compassion.
>
> Judge [] has a really good eye. She could tell when someone was trying to pull one over.

She's a pretty good lady. She's fair. I should have gone to jail a few times but she didn't send me.

She really cares about you. She really makes us her business.

They're [judge and commissioner] really neat people. It's a different setting in family court. You don't get the feeling that they're judging you.

She was great. I liked her. She treated us with respect, instead of like shit.

Good. She lays out the requirements. Tells you how it's gonna be and then it's up to you.

The judge sanctioned [the CWS worker] for not calling me to tell me about some visitation arrangements for my son.

Treatment team member comments included:

(Team member) accountability of treatment providers is good and more intensive by the judge.

I give a lot of credit to Judge [] for her ability to see the big picture and preside over both FTC and dependency matters.

Judge [] is very much invested in the process. Her commitment to clients is evident.

Judge [] integrity and compassion, but also holding clients accountable. I think everyone trusts her.

Chemical Dependency Counselors

When the program began in 2003, the primary treatment counselor was a recovering addict and a mother. When she left the program to take a job at another agency, she was replaced by two graduate students majoring in social work and chemical dependency. The clients reported having a difficult time transitioning to the new counselors, as well as adapting to the new role they had to play as "street-smart" teachers to the "book-smart" counselors. Clients expressed slight frustration at sitting in group, seeing someone high, with the counselor seemingly unaware of it. Statements from various FTC graduates regarding the program treatment counselors follows:

> [First counselor] was great. She was straight up. She knew if you were trying to put one over on her. An addict knows an addict. You know the rationalizations and excuses. It's like ESP versus no ESP.
>
> [Replacement counselor] was just starting out so it was easy to pull the wool over her eyes.
>
> [First counselor] is the best counselor. She helped me with life. I would call her all the time and she talked me through things because she's in recovery herself. [Replacement counselor] is clueless about addiction. She's all textbook. You can't understand addiction unless you've been there.
>
> [Original counselor] is a really cool lady. She is a former addict and had lost custody of her children. She could really relate to what I was going through.
>
> [Original counselor] has been there, done that [addiction, lost children]. She was easy to talk to. She was wonderful, like a friend. I was really, really upset when she left. [Replacement counselor] hasn't been there, she didn't do drugs or alcohol. People in recovery understand better.
>
> I love [original counselor]. She was to the point. She'd call you on your shit. People would come into group high and she'd say, "You, go UA." She'd call me on my stuff that I couldn't see, especially if you've been an addict for years.
> [Original counselor] was the best person. She would fight to the end for us. She was an experienced counselor. [Replacement counselor] was a book counselor. She didn't

> fight for us. She couldn't tell who was just going through the motions and who was working hard.
>
> Some counselors didn't have substance abuse history, and while they were good, they couldn't empathize with what I was going through.

This was an interesting discovery as clients were not asked to identify attributes of a good treatment counselor, yet the majority of graduates identified a counselor in recovery as important to them. When this was brought to the treatment team's attention, it was dismissed out-of-hand as "clients always have a difficult time adjusting to a new counselor."

Interestingly, the "book-smart" male counselor received positive reviews. He was viewed by clients as intelligent, genuine and likable:

> [Counselor] has the coolest sense of humor. He hasn't used, but he's so full of knowledge about addiction. If he doesn't know the answer, he will find it for you.

This counselor established the men's-only group for the program, emphasizing integrity and brotherhood, and facilitated some mixed-gender groups. He also developed customer satisfaction surveys that asked clients which aspects of the program they would change, and which they would keep. Many of the clients named this counselor as an aspect of the program they would keep.

There were generally two treatment counselors and the treatment supervisor on the FTC team.[18] Prior to, or during their course of employment with the program, all of the counselors attained a master's in social work and a certification in chemical dependency counseling. The counselors reported enjoying the opportunity to work with clients for longer courses of treatment. They felt the FTC format allowed them to achieve a more meaningful treatment experience for clients, as compared to the 90-day outpatient programs funded by the state. One treatment counselor described the latter as a "band-aid" approach to

---

[18] In early 2004, the program supported three treatment counselors; however, due to lower than expected program enrollment one of the counselors was reassigned.

treatment – get the client sobered up and out the door. Any problems related to drug use such as the need for sober housing or mental health care are the clients' to solve as there is not enough time for the program to provide the tools or support necessary to change thought patterns or behaviors associated with drug-dependence in the abbreviated programs.

The treatment counselors conducted the FTC program orientation for potential clients and performed the initial Alcohol and Drug Addiction Treatment and Support Act (ADATSA) Assessment to determine addiction history and required level of care. They facilitated the various client treatment groups, and provided one-on-one treatment counseling with the clients.[19] They were responsible for monitoring clients' treatment compliance by establishing individualized weekly UA schedules for clients, conducting the UAs on site, as well as overseeing clients' attendance at required on-site treatment groups and community self-help meetings each week. Clients were generally assigned a treatment counselor based on gender, but could request to work with the other counselor.

Treatment counselors were responsible for writing the bi-weekly court reports on clients that informed the rest of the team on a client's treatment progress. The court reports included the number of required treatment meetings and UAs a client fulfilled, a brief narrative on other emergent issues such as progress in securing housing or employment, or a description of treatment non-compliance. Each client was given an overall assessment by the treatment counselor of "excellent," "satisfactory," or "unsatisfactory" treatment progress. The court reports were based on the counselors' interaction with clients, and confirmation from outside sources, such as housing or health care providers. As treatment counselors only attended family treatment court sessions, they relied on CWS workers for information regarding dependency issues.

During the first year of observation, the team only discussed clients who had "unsatisfactory" treatment progress reports. Clients

---

[19] Treatment groups include: chemical dependency education, anger management, life skills/relapse prevention, and stress management/acupuncture. A process group is ongoing to keep continuity in client interaction. The program has always had specific treatment tracks for women, and in January 2004, started a men's only group.

whose progress was deemed "satisfactory" or "excellent" in sobriety, regardless of parenting or other issues, were not reviewed by the team before court. Often, the treatment counselors, (who focused on the parents' sobriety), had conflicting perceptions of, and recommendations for clients than did the child welfare workers, who focused on the child and examined parenting issues, safe housing, any adult relationships they felt threatened the safety of the child, in addition to parental sobriety. Several treatment team members revealed in interviews that in the first year of the program's operation that treatment counselors sometimes took a client advocacy role best suited for the public defenders. During the second year of team observation, the child welfare workers were more assertive in team meetings about their perceived need to discuss all the clients appearing in court that day (not just the "unsatisfactory" ones, with a more comprehensive dialogue than solely that of sobriety.

Child Welfare Services Workers

In the beginning of the evaluation period in 2004, two child welfare workers and their supervisor were members of the FTC team. A third worker who specialized in tribal dependencies was added the following year to maintain "manageable" worker caseloads. All CWS workers attended all of the FTC team meetings. Clients were assigned to CWS workers based on their Native status, and then by worker caseload. Clients could not request a change in child welfare worker; however, as a rule, when clients were brought into the program they were able to develop a good working relationship and mutual respect with their child welfare worker, and found them to be very helpful. If a client was not invested in their own recovery, they often viewed their child welfare worker as lazy or unhelpful. The FTC team's child welfare supervisor perceived the Department's job as follows: By the time the parents get to her unit, they have had their day in court, and been adjudged responsible for identified behaviors that endangered their child. She encouraged her workers to focus the parent on meeting the court-ordered requirements, and to present themselves as advocates in helping the parent achieve those requirements so that together they could meet the mutual goal of "getting CPS out of their lives as soon as possible."

The child welfare workers reported that it is often easy to initiate a good working relationship with the parent as they get to step in to help the parent work on getting their children back after the other (non-FTC) CPS worker has removed their children from the home. McGee (2000) observes, "The parent's attitude toward the case worker and child welfare department can change from one of antagonism generated from the traditional reporting function of the service provider to a supportive one when it becomes evident at the drug court status hearings that the court and the service providers are trying to work together to help the parent and his or her family" (p. 21).

The child welfare workers' role was to give input on clients who were struggling in treatment, filling in additional background information from the parenting aspect, including observations from parent-child visits, findings from home visits, and reports from service providers who worked with the families. Over the course of the observation period, the child welfare workers provided more of a "big picture" view of the family than the treatment counselors, as the former had access to guardian ad litem reports and other service provider reports (e.g., foster parent, family therapist), and they attended both family treatment court hearings and dependency court hearings, wherein the family dynamics of FTC clients are discussed in more detail.

When clients relapsed, the child welfare workers were the ones who were most familiar with support resources available for families and tried to customize resources to the families' needs.[20] Often, the best treatment team brainstorming was initiated by child welfare workers offering ideas to address a client's need, with the rest of the team debating the pros and cons of each suggestion. Child welfare workers also had the most information regarding potential new clients. They were able to tell the team if the client was formerly CPS-involved, how many children were in the family, and if a significant other or spouse was involved. This information proved key in guiding the team through the decision to approve or deny a potential client's entrance into the FTC program.

---

[20] Service referrals included: therapeutic family counseling, transportation services for children who were removed from the home so they could continue to attend their regular school, child development specialists, and emergency placement facilities.

Assistant Attorneys General

Like the judges in family treatment court, state attorneys who can seamlessly make the switch from a punitive to restorative form of justice are best suited for duties associated with a family treatment court. While the FTC AAGs represent CPS in dependency cases, these state prosecutors brought an immense amount of knowledge with them regarding addiction and parents in crisis. There were two assistant attorneys general on the FTC team who alternated weeks in court, dividing clients into Group A and Group B. Clients were assigned to a group based on AAG caseloads.

The *sine qua non* AAGs endured as the "helping professions" (i.e., CWS and treatment) verbally processed cases at great length during the 1-hour team meeting. With mild to moderate annoyance, the result-oriented attorneys often interrupted discussions asking, *"Okay, so what's the recommendation?"* They were the first, however, to come to a clients' aid who, along with their addiction, were victims of domestic violence. The AAGs frequently provided the impetus for the team to examine and update program policy, asking the "What if?" questions regarding the imposition of sanctions, or the team's decision to allow both a domestic violent perpetrator and victim into the FTC program together.

Clients remarked on the more positive perception they had of the AAGs as they began to see them regularly in the court setting. One client affirmed:

> The first time we met her (AAG) was at the shelter care hearing. I didn't like her because she took my child. But then you start seeing her every week in court. I never felt there was a tone that she was against me or judging me. I realized she was just doing her job.

Another client stated:

> The AAGs are strict. They love to see you do well, but they hold you accountable. They're not there to hang out or waste time. They're very professional. You know when you're there (in court) it's serious, it's not a 3-ring circus.

Public Defense Attorneys

National Drug Court Institute Executive Director Karen Freeman-Wilson notes, "Since the inception of the drug court movement in America, arguably no player on the drug court team – be it judge, prosecuting attorney or treatment provider – has struggled more with his or her own identity than the defense attorney. The desires of the treatment team to hold parents accountable and the desires of the drug court client are, at times, conflicting and can seemingly put the defense attorney in a box with no way out" (2003, p. 3). The tension between the need for increased judicial flexibility and authority on the one hand, and the risks inherent in this same flexibility and authority on the other, requires a defense attorney participating in the drug court system to strike a constant balance between acquiescing to informal procedures and practices that would not be tolerated in the traditional criminal court system, and trying to protect the client from the severe punishments that constantly remain available (p. 3). These circumstances were highly prevalent for public defenders on the FTC team.

When the program was established in 2003, members of the public defender's office wondered if this was simply a faster way for CPS to terminate parental rights. In an effort to negotiate program buy-in by the public defenders, the AAGs acquiesced to their condition of no jail time as a sanction. A few months into the program, jail time was added as a sanction as a result of client input, with full team approval. One program founding member explained:

> The clients at the time told us, "If you had sent me to jail, I would still be in this program." After jail was included as a sanction, clients told FTC team members that going to jail straightened them out.

Chief Public Defender for Los Angeles County, Michael P. Judge (1995) observed, "In family treatment court, the goals of representation are revised so that a traditional attorney focus on "avoiding or minimizing loss of liberty and the imposition of other sanctions" becomes instead a focus on helping to effectuate "long term general lifestyle outcomes." In short, defense counsel is no longer primarily responsible for giving voice to the distinct perspective of the client's experience in what remains a coercive setting. Rather, defense counsel becomes part of a treatment team working with others to insure that outcomes, viewed from the perspective of the institutional players and not the individual defendant, are in the defendant's best interests (p. 1). During one of the FTC team meetings, the public defender commented (half-jokingly) "*I told my client I don't have a lot of say back here.*" He voiced concern about losing all credibility with clients if he cannot haggle over sanctions.

Freeman-Wilson (2003) identified specific ways that family treatment court defense attorneys must continue zealous advocacy for their clients, noting that the bulk of a family treatment court defense attorney's time is spent on treatment compliance issues. As a result, drug court defense attorneys must be trained to understand and assist their clients in addressing all compliance issues that may arise. This includes thoroughly investigating, and appropriately addressing, the impact of alleged noncompliance. It also includes assisting clients in explaining their position and asserting available defenses for non-compliance. For example, counsel must help to provide a coherent framework for any explanation that might involve culturally confounding circumstances and/or co-occurring disorder exacerbations. Counsel must also understand, and be able to present to the court, the reliability limits of individual drug tests (e.g., potential false positive reads, standard error of measurement of the procedure, exceeding the minimum testable quantity, or shoddy lab procedures), and ensure that sanctions remain realistic and appropriate to the case at hand, taking into account a client's multi-dimensional needs. Inappropriate sanctions can be self-defeating (p. 28). One FTC graduate recalled:

> The second sanction, they (FTC team) said I missed a UA so they sanctioned me. I had to do jury box. Then they checked and I hadn't missed it. There's two different standards – [one for the clients and one for the FTC team members]. It's way less for the team.

Like the FTC AAGs, the FTC public defenders have caseloads outside of FTC. Program clients were assigned to public defenders based on workload, but also to avoid conflict of interest issues when couples entered the program together, or when the public defender represented a spouse or significant other of an FTC client on other legal matters. Their caseloads and trial schedules were so intense that they relied heavily on the FTC treatment counselors and child welfare workers to provide them with supplemental information about their clients, and possible supportive services. During interviews, the public defenders often stated their appreciation for this information sharing aspect of the program.

One FTC public defender noted:

> In non-FTC cases, it's more contentious between the public defenders and the CWS workers. Plus, we get the plum clients in FTC.

> The public defenders are here for the marginal cases. We have to "sell" the clients' best interest to them, make them see what is in their best interest.[21]

Graduates noted that if you followed the program, you had very limited need for your public defender.

The public defenders often served as the lone advocate for parents who had relapsed or otherwise violated their treatment agreement when the rest of the team members became frustrated and were ready to discharge the client. Team members were willing to listen to the public defenders' argument, but as a rule they remained firm about holding clients accountable for their program violations through the imposition of sanctions. If the team could not reach a consensus on how to handle a given situation, the AAG presented the team recommendation (*sans* the public defender) to the court, and the public defender typically appealed to the judge for leniency.

The first two public defenders in the program received mixed reviews by program clients. Compliments included:

> He was nice. He returned my calls.

---

[21] See Blumberg (1967) describing defense attorneys as cooperative players with judges and prosecutors who influence client choices to serve systemic efficiency.

Criticisms included:

> He didn't do anything to help me keep my child.
>
> He rambled on in court and never really said anything.

In the second observation year, one of the FTC public defenders was reassigned and replaced by a very 'spirited' public defender whom the clients raved about. They liked that she would stand up to CWS workers and treatment counselors when they wanted to impose additional conditions on clients from those stated in their Order of Dependency, and how she would make an argument for their concerns in court. During one FTC team meeting, the treatment counselors asserted that a client needed to secure structured housing in order to successfully complete the treatment program. The public defender pointed out that "structured" housing was not in the court order, so the client should not have to comply with it. The treatment counselors countered that structured housing is part of the client's treatment plan, to which the client had signed their consent. During one team meeting, the public defender commented that there was confusion by clients who felt they did not have to comply with certain treatment recommendations because they were in a *voluntary* program. Team members explained that while the FTC program is voluntary, treatment recommendations are court-ordered and as such, are required.

While in theory public defenders should be the most zealous advocate for their clients, in practice the treatment counselors advocated for the treatment needs of the participant, CWS advocated for the parenting needs of the client (e.g., visitation, parenting classes, transportation, housing), and the defense attorneys advocated for what the client wanted to do regarding their treatment plan.

Surprisingly, through team meeting observations it became clear that knowledge regarding the nature of drug addiction was not a prerequisite for defense attorneys assigned to the FTC team. During team discussions, it was common for a defense attorney to ask questions of the team about the progression or manifestation of addiction, calling into question their ability to adequately advocate for the needs of their clients. Defense attorneys would also frequently vacillate between asking the treatment counselors and CWS for ideas on appropriate referrals for clients who were struggling in the program, and frequently arguing against inpatient or transitional housing recommendations made by treatment or CWS based on client objections to the referral.

McGee (2000) notes, “In many instances, "red flags" must be either validated or subsequently ruled out as manifestations of a substance abuse problem. This is especially true where the use of drugs is not overtly present but, instead, suggested through other lifestyle conduct” (p. 7). The FTC treatment counselors and public defenders often argued this very point. Treatment counselors would assert that certain client behaviors such as lying about who they were associating was an ‘old behavior’ indicating drug use, and should be dealt with by the treatment team. The public defenders would argue that such client associations were not addressed in the court order of dependency, so the client was not required to divulge them to the treatment team. In one case, a client had an unsatisfactory progress report and had received one sanction two months previously. The team recommended twenty hours of community service for the second sanction that typically earned five hours of community service. In court, the judge asked why the team recommended this severe of sanction for an unsatisfactory report for only one missed group. CWS and the AAG explained it was for “lifestyle choices” the client was making – alluding to the client fraternizing with using partners, and then lying to treatment team members about it. The judge reduced the sanction to ten hours of community service, highlighting the need for the client to get honest if he/she was to ultimately succeed in recovery.

Another area where the FTC public defenders asserted themselves was in the distinction between treatment issues and dependency issues. For example, during an FTC team meeting, CWS stated a concern regarding a parent missing visitation appointments with their children, among other issues regarding child welfare. When the team began discussing possible sanctions for the client skirting around program compliance, the public defender argued:

> We can’t sanction clients for missed visits. Those are dependency issues, not treatment issues.

At times, however, the public defender's zealous advocacy worked against the client. Much of the debate in team meetings centered around adhering to, or deviating from the established graduated sanctions. These discussions proved to be the workgroup dynamic at its best (See Eisenstein & Jacob, 1991: Ch. 2 & 3). Team members were willing to engage in insightful discussion and thoughtful consideration of the arguments for and against a particular client.

Ironically, team members would not always stay on the same side of the issue, sometimes arguing the opposing position they supported just a moment or a week earlier. The dialogue regarding sanctions was the most comprehensive of any topic discussed by the team. In one instance, the majority of the team members recommended jail time for a non-compliant client. The public defender persuasively argued that jail was not the next step in the graduated sanctions schedule, so the team recommendation changed to increased community service hours. When the public defender proudly took this recommendation to the client, the client said they would have preferred jail time because it required less of a time commitment than the proposed community service hours, and therefore less likely to interfere with the client's work schedule.

Court-Appointed Special Advocates (CASAs)/Guardian ad litems (GALs)

During the initial shelter care hearing of a child dependency case, the family court judge (also the family treatment court judge in this jurisdiction) would appoint a Guardian ad litem (GAL). The GAL was primarily responsible for gathering information regarding the dependent children, their family, living conditions, and other social environments such as school or daycare. The GAL interviewed various family members, friends and service providers to develop an informational report for the court, and make recommendations on whether or not the child should become dependent. The GAL's solitary role is to consider the "best interest of the child," whereas the CWS worker's job is to advocate for the families by setting them up with services (e.g., parenting classes, family counseling, etc.) to facilitate family preservation.

The county CASA department had four GAL staff members and four CASA volunteers who managed approximately 30 FTC children, in addition to a non-FTC child caseload. FTC required GALs to write reports every three months, as opposed to every six months for non-FTC clients. When caseloads were too great, GAL staff members were more likely to drop an FTC case (as opposed to a non-FTC case) because FTC clients "have more eyes on them" (i.e., the judge and other treatment team members).

Clients who did well in the program said they only saw their GAL once or twice in the beginning of the program and did not have strong opinions about them either way. The GAL supervisor stated, "*They* [FTC parents] *almost don't need a GAL because the court is watching them so closely*." Clients who struggled in the program did not necessarily see their GALs more often, however they had very unfavorable views of the GALs, generally believing the GALS were the primary reason for any delays in returning their children.

Treatment Team Issues

As with all collaborative endeavors, family treatment court comes with some built-in conflict. The separate and distinct foci of individual team members could, at times, be used by FTC clients to their own advantage. Treatment team members described how, early on in the program, clients tried to "play" one team member against another. As client and treatment counselor relationships developed, some clients would report distorted versions of CWS requirements in an attempt to induce their treatment counselors to intervene with the assigned child welfare worker on the client's behalf. This created a significant amount of discord between CWS workers and treatment counselors. To their credit, instead of becoming increasingly distant, the two agencies began holding monthly meetings with only their agencies present (no other treatment team members were invited), to improve their working relationship. Interestingly, when the public defenders became aware of what they viewed were "secret" meetings during discussion at a team meeting, it caused some mistrust of treatment counselors and CWS team members by the public defenders. The public defenders felt there was a danger of CWS workers and treatment counselors "staffing" client cases without anyone being present who represented the client.

CWS workers and treatment counselors stopped meeting for a while and then covertly resumed, feeling it a necessary process to achieve optimal communication between the two agencies. These meetings did achieve their purpose, creating an increased level of trust between the two groups and ultimately resulting in the three-way meeting innovation discussed previously with the child welfare workers, treatment counselors and all incoming clients. This policy effectively minimized the havoc created by clients trying to "work" the system and play one team member against another.

One child welfare worker observed:

> It has really helped since treatment and CWS have been meeting outside the attorneys' presence. We've cleared some lines and clarified roles. CWS felt that treatment was overstepping the bounds in case planning, because that is not their role. Their role is the chemical dependency treatment of the client. We're constantly talking about how we're feeling – treatment getting roped into stuff by clients. Treatment was taking everything the clients say as gospel. We (FTC team) need to really be aware of being played off of each other by the clients. If we get too much into the caretaking role, we get played. The client's main advocate should be their attorney in court.

Another area where the diversified team member's focus caused team discord was when the public defenders would relay the treatment team's sanction recommendation to a client before going into court, then stand up in court and argue against the team recommendation based on their subsequent conversation with the client. Part of the dissention by the treatment team members was the public defenders not informing any of them of the new game plan prior to court, to provide them the opportunity to assess the veracity of the new information and jointly deliberate on an adjusted recommendation, if necessary. Often, when the public defender would raise the client's objection in court, the judge would turn to the other team members for additional information and they were generally unprepared to respond due to having just heard this new information themselves. One treatment team member stated in this regard:

> I don't like it when [public defender] comes into court and presents this off-the-wall motion and makes the team look like idiots.

The other problem with this tactic, from the team members' view, was that this course of action sometimes proved an effective stall tactic from the imposition of immediate sanctions until all parties had ample time to investigate; the client got to call the shots under these circumstances. This is not to say that clients were allowed to stall with *any* excuse; however, the judge was willing to give the benefit of the doubt to a client with a plausible explanation for not meeting some program requirements. This resulted in team members sometimes feeling they wasted their time staffing the client's case.

A rift that sometimes arose in team meetings was the attorney-client relationship between the Attorney General's Office and CPS. One AAG described her role as:

> Representing DCFS (Department of Child and Family Services), to work with the Department to make sure whatever task they're doing gets done, and to present any information the Department thinks is important to the judge.

During several meetings the CWS supervisor would refer to the AAG as "our attorney," even stating at times "*I need to consult with our attorney*," indicating a desire to speak out of the presence of the rest of the team members. These statements stirred up issues surrounding team member equality and maintaining open communication among team members. Interestingly, this CWS mentality changed dramatically as the treatment counselors and CWS workers developed a better working relationship through their exclusive meetings.

Another treatment team issue that generated debate was that of differing views on the appropriate level of involvement of the GALs in treatment court. Because this program consisted largely of volunteers, the county GAL office elected not to require the FTC GALs to attend weekly or bi-weekly treatment court sessions. Instead, one of the GAL supervisors attended FTC team meetings and court hearings to relay any pertinent information back to the GALs. Consequently, the GAL supervisors did not play a very active role in either the treatment team meetings or treatment court hearings. Because the family treatment court judge also served as the dependency court judge, where GALs do attend court without fail, this exclusion did not seem to negatively affect the clients in any way. Some team members expressed a desire to have the GALs play a more active role in FTC in order to make the children's perspective more visible in this arena.

This topic related to another issue with which the treatment team struggled – namely, broadening the focus of program clients to issues outside of recovery. One team member noted:

> In the beginning, we (the FTC team) were so focused on the parents. It was like, "Where are the kids in this?" But the dependency review hearings every three months [for FTC clients] helps us hear from service providers other than substance abuse treatment.

During the first year of treatment team meeting observations, the vast majority of team discussions were centered around how the parents were progressing in treatment. One treatment counselor stated:

> Parenting doesn't necessarily need to be addressed in chemical dependency.

The child welfare workers seldom offered much information to the team members about the children of program clients during team meetings. Child welfare worker interviews revealed a feeling of frustration with not discussing the children more fully during team meetings. They felt pressed for time during the one-hour team meeting and did not want to curtail necessary treatment discussions. Further, if a client was doing well in treatment, the rest of the team did not see a need to deliberate on the client. Eventually the issue surfaced regarding the need to discuss the family as a whole during team meetings, not just the parent's progress in treatment, in order to provide all team members a more comprehensive picture of the client. As a result, even when clients were receiving 'satisfactory' or 'excellent' assessments in treatment, CWS may or may not have provided a differing account of the client regarding their parenting progress. This change allowed for better communication and helped develop trust among treatment team members. It also provided more detailed explanations to all clients in court as to why families were reuniting at different rates, despite their equal success in treatment. It is important to note that child welfare workers did not provide copies of clients' Individual Service and Safety Plan (ISSP), or the client psychological evaluation (if one was done) to treatment counselors until near the end of the second year of the program's operation. Once this procedure was in place, the treatment counselors had a more comprehensive picture of clients outside of their sobriety issues.

Similarly, the team often debated the assessment and requirement of "non-treatment" issues. For example, child welfare workers would push for counseling for a parent to help them resolve abuse issues they suffered as a child that workers believed significantly interfered with the parent's child-rearing abilities. One FTC treatment provider observed:

> CWS believes you can mandate everything. Treatment counselors believe if someone isn't willing or ready to address an issue, it won't help to make them go to treatment. [Making them address] it can even cause a relapse. You need to be careful about ordering services.

Many times CWS workers would express concern in team meetings that the inability of the parent to address these "non-treatment" issues stymied the Department's ability to recommend reunification out of a genuine concern for the child. CWS workers consistently pointed out to treatment counselors and the rest of the team that if left unresolved, such issues could cause the client to relapse, and more often than not, convinced the team that their "recommendation" would be in the best interest of the family.

The members of the FTC team, while steadfast delegates of their respective agencies' mission and goals, were each uniquely capable of advancing their concerns, while thoughtfully weighing and incorporating views of other team members into a customized solution for clients.

This process evaluation facilitated a more fully informed outcome evaluation, discussed in the next chapter.

CHAPTER 10

Family Treatment Court Outcomes

The outcome evaluation for this family treatment court includes the first group of FTC graduates from October 2003, through clients entering the program by December 31, 2005, or a concurrent time period for eligible individuals who chose not to enter the program (i.e., the comparison group). This chapter discusses the following findings:

- Client Program Retention and Completion
- Family Reunification
- Continued Parental Drug Involvement
- The FTC Program's Application to Life Course Theory
- Findings Regarding Stated Hypotheses

While this study does include a comparison group, it should be noted that this is a quasi-experimental research design. Study subjects included a convenience sample of individuals who were CPS-involved due to substance abuse and who called the FTC treatment provider to inquire further about the program from 2002 through 2005. Study subjects subsequently self-selected whether or not to enter the program, thus assigning themselves to either the treatment or comparison group. Subjects in the treatment group were further divided between program graduates and non-completers (i.e., the "early out" group).

The early out group consisted of individuals who opted out of the program, and those who were discharged from the program.

FTC Client Retention and Completion

Fifty percent of clients who entered the program during the study period graduated. Annual rates of graduation for clients who opted into the program from 2002 through 2005 ranged from a high of 80% for the 2002 cohort, to a low of 26% the following year.

Table 10.1: FTC Graduation Rates by Cohort

2002 Cohort	80% (8/10)
2003 Cohort	26% (9/34)
2004 Cohort	65% (13/20)
2005 Cohort	58% (14/24)
Overall Average	**50% (44/88)**

During interviews, team members expressed remorse and disappointment at accepting clients into the program early on (2003) in an effort to build up the program, when some of these individuals were not necessarily a good fit for the services provided by the program. Specifically, clients with mental health issues or learning difficulties (e.g., suicidal, developmental disabilities) that once the program assisted them with sobriety, they could not receive the support necessary to help them sustain the level of parenting skills CWS deemed necessary before returning their children to their care. After some difficult, unsuccessful cases, team members became more selective in client admissions into the program.

Client Retention Rates and Comparative Treatment Duration

The program was able to retain 53 of 88 (60%) clients in treatment for more than nine months.[22] The following table depicts the length of stay in treatment for each of the three study groups. FTC graduates averaged 55 weeks of treatment – significantly longer than the treatment duration of program non-completers (19 weeks) and the comparison group (8 weeks).

[22] Less than eight and more than nine months was a natural dividing line that occurred in this data set.

Table 10.2: Comparative Treatment Durations (in Weeks)

	Mean	Range	Mode
Graduates (44)	55	45 - 76	51
Early Outs (44)	19	0 - 70	10
Comparison (36)	8	0 - 50	0

The majority of the comparison group (20 of 36) did not engage in treatment at all after CPS removed their children from their care. For the early out group, 57% (25 of 44) stayed in treatment for 10 weeks or less.

CPS files indicate that parents in the comparison group also routinely missed visitation appointments with their children, and UA screening appointments to confirm their abstinence from drug use, regardless of their participation in a drug treatment program. In addition, many of these parents did not have a stable residence or contact number where treatment counselors or social service providers could reach them. The next section examines the statistical predictors of successful completion of the FTC and family reunification.

Predictors of Program Completion and of Family Reunification

One of the main objectives of a family treatment court is family reunification. Statistical analysis was conducted to test the hypothesis that FTC clients are more likely than non-participants or non-completers to reunify with their children at some point. Due to the small number of study subjects (124), several variables of interest were either categorized or dummy coded to achieve large enough subgroups to permit statistical analysis. Table 10.3 depicts how variables were coded for purposes of analysis.

For both outcome variables, the Pearson's chi-square test of independence was used to identify variables that reached statistical significance as predictors of both graduation and family reunification (See Tables 10.4 and 10.6). The Uncertainty Coefficient (UC) was used to calculate the percent by which each statistically significant, independent variable reduced prediction uncertainty in the dependent variables. The Uncertainty Coefficient was chosen over the commonly used lambda measure because it takes into account the entire distribution rather than just the modal distribution used in the lambda calculation of the proportionate reduction in error.

Table 10.3: Variable Coding Methods

Parent Gender	0 = Male 1 = Female
Parent Race	0 = Non-Caucasian; 1 = Caucasian
Length of Dependency*	1 = ≤ 12 months 2 = 13 – 24 months 3 = 25 – 36 months 4 = 37 – 49 months
Parent Age Group*	1 = 20 - 25 years 2 = 26 – 30 years 3 = 31 – 35 years 4 = 36 years or older
Program Status	0 = Graduate 1 = Comparison Group 2 = Early Out Group
Parent Continued Drug Use **Employed @ Program Exit** **Automobile Available** **Previous CPS Involvement** **Personal Residence** **Married/Committed Relationship** **≥ High School Education**	Dichotomous (0 = No; 1 = Yes)

gory is used as the reference category in both instances.

Table 10.4: Significant Predictors of Program Graduation

	Chi-Square	df	Uncertainty Coefficient	Cramer's V
Parent Continued Drug Use	22.603*	1	.145	.430
Parent Age Group	10.372*	3	.064	.289
Automobile Available[a]	9.060*	1	.059	.278
Previous CPS Involvement	7.468*	1	.045	.245
Length of Dependency[b]	8.033*	3	.063	.274
Personal Residence	4.827*	1	.031	.197
Employed at Program Exit	4.484*	1	.027	.191
Parent Race	3.257	1	.022	.162
$\geq$High School Graduate[c]	2.963	1	.021	.166
Parent Gender	1.892	1	.011	.124
Married/Committed Relationship	.347	1	.002	.053

Note: N = 124 *p<.05

[a] 7 cases had missing data on the Automobile Available variable. All 7 cases were from the early out and comparison groups, comprising 9% (7/80) of the non-graduate group.

[b] 17 cases had missing data on the Length of Dependency variable. All 17 cases were from the early out and comparison groups, comprising 20% (17/80) of the non-graduate group.

[c] 16 cases had missing data for the Parent Education Level: 13 (36%) of the comparison group, and 3 (7%) of the early out group. Combined, the missing data comprises 20% (16/80) of the non-graduate group. A chi square analysis omitting the comparison group from the analysis (and reducing the missing data from 20% to 7% on the Education Level data) also resulted in the Education Level as not significantly associated with graduation from the FTC program.

In addition to estimating the proportionate reduction in error using the Uncertainty Coefficient, the strength of association between the dichotomous dependent variables – program graduation and family reunification – and the identified statistically significant independent variables, was assessed using the Cramer's V measure of association. Cramer's V was chosen due to its customary use as a chi square-based measure of nominal association. Independent variables that were assessed for their predictive power relating to program graduation are listed in Table 10.4.

As depicted in Table 10.4, parents' continued drug use, previous CPS involvement, length of current dependency, and indicators of some material comforts (e.g., access to a car, employment, stable housing) appear to have some predictive value in program graduation. Using these same variables, logistic regression was utilized to develop a prediction model for the dependent variable graduate/not graduate. Backward elimination was used to select independent variables included in the binomial logistic regression model featured in Table 10.5.

Table 10.5: Logistic Regression Model Predicting FTC Graduation

Variables	FULL MODEL R^2 = .567*		TRIMMED MODEL R^2 = .476*		CHI SQUARE SIG. MODEL R^2 = .453*	
	(B) (S.E.)	Exp(B)	(B) (S.E.)	Exp(B)	(B) (S.E.)	Exp(B)
Dependency Category 1 (≤ 12 months)[a]	.548 (1.773)	1.730	.294 (1.701)	1.341	.286 (1.693)	1.331
Dependency Category 2 (13-24 months)	4.241* (1.750)	69.475	2.754* (1.379)	15.709	2.529 (1.379)	12.547
Dependency Category 3 (25-36 months)	3.310 (1.794)	27.382 .679	2.338 (1.483)	10.361 .806	2.364 (1.484)	10.638
Parent Gender	-387 (.8580)		-216 (.705)		-----	-----
Parent Race (Caucasian/Non-Caucasian)	2.646* (1.204)	14.104	1.276 (.912)	3.583	-----	-----

Table 10.5 (Continued): Logistic Regression Model Predicting FTC Graduation

Variables	FULL MODEL R^2 = .567*		TRIMMED MODEL R^2 = .476*		CHI SQUARE SIG. MODEL R^2 = .453*	
	(B) (S.E.)	Exp(B)	(B) (S.E.)	Exp(B)	(B) (S.E.)	Exp(B)
Personal Residence	-.127 (.686)	.881	.548 (.545)	1.730	.499 (.535)	1.646
Parent Married/ Committed Relationship	-.835 (.762)	.434	-.482 (.610)	.618	-----	-----
Automobile Available	.770 (.618)	2.160	.435 (.537)	1.545	.443 (.532)	1.557
High School Education	-.763 (.790)	.466	-----	-----	-----	-----
Employed at Program Exit	.958 (.783)	2.608. 079	.049 (.609)	1.050 .192	.021 (.599)	1.021 .175
Parent Age Group 1 (20-25 years old)[b]	-2.537 (1.492)		-1.651 (.964)		-1.745 (9.36)	
Parent Age Group 2 (26-30 years old)	-4.000* (1.450)	.018	-2.409* (1001)	.090	-2.264* (.979)	.104
Parent Age Group 3 (31-35 years old)	-2.801* (1.254)	.061	-1.833* (.849)	.160	-1.719* (.826)	179

Table 10.5 (Continued): Logistic Regression Model Predicting FTC Graduation

Variables	FULL MODEL R^2 = .567*		TRIMMED MODEL R^2 = .476*		CHI SQUARE SIG. MODEL R^2 = .453*	
	(B) (S.E.)	Exp(B)	(B) (S.E.)	Exp(B)	(B) (S.E.)	Exp(B)
Previous CPS Involvement	-1.806* (.754)	.164*	-1.275* (6.09)	.280	-1.312* (.592)	.269
Parent Continued Drug Use	-1.183 (.675)	.306	-1.688* (.569)	.185	-1.731* (.559)	.177
Constant	-1.022 (2.029)	.360	-.758 (1.751)	.469	.160 (1.41)	1.173

Note: N = 124 *p<.05.

[a] The reference category for length of child dependency case is 37 to 49 months.

[b] The reference category for parent age is ≥36 years old at program entry (or concurrent time for comparison group).

The full model above includes all of the variables that achieved statistical significance in the chi square test, plus demographic variables commonly included as predictive measures in the drug court literature (i.e., parent race, gender, education level, and relationship to partner.) (See Family Drug Court Activity Update, 2000). The full model produced a significant chi square of 47.607.

A trimmed model (included in Table 10.5) was generated for two reasons: First, as explained in the preceding footnote, 36% (13) of the comparison group had missing data for the parent education variable. To address this, a chi square analysis of parent education as a predictor of program graduation was run using only the graduate and early out groups (where only 7% of the data was missing for the parent education variable). In both instances, [including and omitting the comparison group] the parent education variable passed the chi square test of independence in relation to program graduation – it was not predictive of graduation from the FTC program (the second reason it was removed from the logistic regression model). The trimmed model, that excluded the parent education variable was a slightly less robust model (R^2 = .476 versus .567 in the full model), but still achieved significance with a chi square score of 43.370.

It is important to note that removing the parent education variable from the full model affected the significance levels of both *parent race* and *parent continued drug use* as predictor variables. With the absence of parent education, parent race became a statistically non-significant predictor of program graduation, and parents' continued drug use became a statistically significant predictor of program graduation. It is difficult to assess whether race is predictive in this evaluation as only five individuals (four African American, one Hawaiian/Pacific Islander – all in the early out group) did not identify themselves as either Caucasian or Native American. Perhaps slightly more telling is that out of ten Native Americans in the study group, only two graduated from the FTC program. Of the remaining eight, three opted not to enter the program, and five entered, but did not complete the program. However, a much larger, more diverse cohort is necessary to assess parents' race accurately as a predictive measure.

The parents' *continued drug use* variable remained a significant predictor of program graduation through several permutations of logistic regression models. When only the variables that reached chi square significance were included in another trimmed model, all remained significant predictors of program graduation, generating an R^2 of .453, and a critical chi square of 40.833 (included in Table 10.5).

To summarize, variables that consistently predicted graduation from FTC were:

- Parent Age Group 2 (26-30 years old)
- Parent Age Group 3 (31-35 years old)
- Previous CPS Involvement
- Parents' Continued Drug Use

While the 13-24 month dependency (category 2) variable was significant in the full model and the trimmed model (i.e., omitting the parent education variable), it failed to reach significance when it was included in a logistic regression analysis with only variables that achieved critical prediction scores in the chi square analysis. This dependency category variable also lost its predictive power when it was included in a logistic regression that contained only the four variables listed above – those that consistently achieved statistical significance in a logistic regression predicting program graduation. This result may be due to the fact that 63% (67/107) of the dependencies for this data set were closed in 13-24 months (the dependency category 2 length), and were evenly split between graduates (33) and non-graduates (34).

The same statistical analysis used to identify predictive measures for program graduation was also used to identify significant indicators of family reunification. The results of that analysis are presented in Table 10.6.

Table 10.6: Significant Predictors of Family Reunification

	Chi-Square	df	Uncertainty Coefficient	Cramer's V
Program Status	53.350*	2	.340	.656
Parent Continued Drug Use	43.937*	1	.280	.600
Length of Dependency	18.169*	3	.140	.412
Automobile Available	10.871*	1	.069	.305
Employed at Program Exit	8.979*	1	.053	.270
Parent Age Group	7.828*	3	.048	.251
Personal Residence	7.440*	1	.045	.245
Parent Race	3.623	1	.023	.171
Previous CPS Involvement	2.297	1	.014	.136
Parent Gender	1.733	1	.010	.118

Table 10.6 (Continued): Significant Predictors of Family Reunification

	Chi-Square	df	Uncertainty Coefficient	Cramer's V
Relative/Foster Care Emergency Placement	1.485	1	.009	.109
≥ High School Education[a]	.774	1	.005	.085
Married/Committed Relationship	.081	1	.000	.026

Note: N = 124 *p<.05

[a] 16 cases (13 comparison; 3 early out group) had data missing for the Parent Education Level variable, comprising 13% of the total study group. A chi square analysis omitting the comparison group from the analysis (and reducing the missing data from 13% to 3% on the Education Level data) also resulted in the Parent Education Level variable not being significantly associated with family reunification.

The chi square analysis indicated that a parent's program status (i.e., control group, early out, graduate), their continuation or cessation of drug use, the length of their dependency case, their age, and possession of some material comforts (e.g., access to automobile, stable housing, employment) all affected a family's likelihood of reunification. A logistic regression analysis including these variables (Table 10.7) produced a statistically significant model with an R^2 of .778 and a critical chi square score of 99.142.[23]

As illustrated in Table 10.7, parents who were older (age 31-35), who graduated from the program (and therefore had a permanent residence as required by the program), were able to refrain from drug use, and who had their children placed with relatives (as opposed to a foster home) were more likely to be reunified with their children and have their child dependency cases dismissed.

[23] The 'Dependency Length' variable was omitted from the logistic regression analysis as it was not predictive of family reunification and served only to contaminate the model.

Table 10.7: Logistic Regression Model Predicting Family Reunification[a]

	B (S.E.)	Exp(B)
Parent Age Group 1 (20-25 years old)	1.768 (1.343)	5.862
Parent Age Group 2 (26-30 years old)	-.451 (1.136)	.637
Parent Age Group 3 (31-35 years old)	2.115* (1.075)	8.286
Parent Race	-.212 (1.054)	.809
Program Status 1 (Comparison Group)b	-3.387* (.963)	.034
Program Status 2 (Early Outs)	-4.486* (1.074)	.011
Personal Residence	1.962* (.925)	7.113
Married/Committed Relationship	.264 (.838)	1.303
Availability of Automobile	-4.65 (.817)	.628
Employed at Program Exit	.240 (.916)	1.271
Parent Continued Drug Use	-3.770* (.984)	.023
Previous CPS Involvement	.651 (.920)	1.917
Relative or Foster Care Emergency Placement[c]	1.655* (.816)	5.233
Parent Gender	.271 (.966)	1.311
Constant	.755 (1.798)	2.127

Note: N = 124 $^*p<.05$

[a] The reference category for parent age is ≥36 years old at program entry (or concurrent time for comparison group).

[b] The reference category for Program Status is graduation. Program Status was used in the analysis instead of the dichotomous graduate/not graduate variable because it added a third category by splitting the comparison group and the early outs from the graduates, and proved to be a slightly better predictor of family reunification than did graduate/not graduate variable (Naglekerke R^2 .778 versus .776 for graduate/not graduate).

[c] Foster Home = 0; Relative Placement = 1

Table 10.8 summarizes family reunification rates by parent end status: graduates, opt outs, discharges, and the comparison group. As demonstrated, 86% of graduates had their children returned to them, versus 25% of the opt outs, 22% of the comparison group, and 11% of the discharged parents.[24]

Table 10.8 also demonstrates that FTC graduates comprised 72% (38/53) of parents who were reunified with their children, versus 15% (8/53) for the comparison group, 7% for the opted out group, and 6% for the discharged group. As further depicted in Table 10.8, parents who did not participate in or complete the FTC program were far more likely to lose their parental rights related to this dependency.

Table 10.8: Reunification/Parental Rights by Program Status

	Graduate	Discharged	Opted Out	Control Group
Percent Reunited w/Children	86%	11%	25%	22%
Number Reunited w/Children (53/124)	38/44	3/28	4/16	8/36
Percent Losing Parental Rights	7%	54%	58%	38%

Comparative Child Dependency Duration

The promise or perception of shorter out-of-home placements was a much contested issue in the FTC. In the beginning of the program, team members would pledge faster return of children whose parents entered the FTC program. Conversely, potential clients would decline participation in the program, believing it would take longer for their children to be returned to them. Findings from this research revealed comparable average dependency durations for graduates versus the comparison groups. These findings are reported in Table 10.9.

---

[24] The 'early out' group was split in this instance to highlight the noticeably different findings on this variable between those who opted out of the program and those who were discharged from the program.

Table 10.9: Number of Months Dependency Open*

	Mean	Median	Mode	Range
Opted Out (12)	19	19	13 & 20	12-32
Comparison (30)	19	18	13	5-35
Graduate (43)	21	20	20	11-49
Discharged (22)	26	25	43	10-48

*17 cases (14%) in the study group remained open at the time the CPS records were pulled in late 2006. Therefore, the length of their dependencies are missing from this research.

Although graduates had comparable dependency durations to the comparison and opt out groups, recall that 86% of graduates had their children returned to them, while only 25% of opt outs, 22% of the comparison group, and 11% of discharged individuals were reunited with their children. These findings provide evidence that this family treatment court did serve as a change point for those who successfully completed the program. As described by life course theorists, the graduates' life trajectories largely transitioned from that of addiction and threatened loss of their children to that of a parent who has learned how to cope with life challenges and celebrate by healthier means that exclude drug use. Conversely, the comparison group and early outs from the program essentially remained on their addiction life course, ultimately resulting in the loss of their children.

While not statistically significant, it is noteworthy that the majority of graduates came to the attention of CPS via law enforcement, while the majority of the comparison group was reported to CPS by a neighbor, family member, childcare or school worker (see Table 10.10). The involvement of law enforcement in this early stage may have provided impetus for substance-abusing parents to successfully complete the FTC program.

This research also examined potential indicators for subsequent CPS involvement and continued parental drug use. Bivariate analysis of subsequent CPS involvement and continued parental drug use was conducted to identify potential predictors, as described earlier in this chapter. The results are shown in Table 10.11.

Table 10.10: Method of CPS Detection for Substance Abusing Parents

	Graduated	Early Out	Control Group
Childbirth/Prenatal Exam	12	14	10
Neighbor/Family/Childcare or School	12	14	13
Law Enforcement	15	11	6
Other Health Care Personnel	5	5	7

Subsequent CPS Involvement and Continued Parental Drug Use

Table 10.11: Significant Predictors of Subsequent CPS Involvement

	Chi-Square	df	Uncertainty Coefficient	Cramer's V
Client End Status[a]	14.813*	3	.166	.403
Length of Dependency	8.727*	3	.075	.315
Child Placed with Relatives[b]	5.591*	1	.049	.248

Note: N = 124 *p<.05

[a] Client End Status designates one of four possible categories for study subjects: graduated, opted out, discharged, or did not opt in.

[b] Child ultimately placed with parents or extended family members = 1; Child ultimately placed with non-relatives = 0

Other variables that were evaluated using the chi square test for independence but found not to be statistically significant predictors of subsequent CPS involvement included:

- Parent Age
- Parent Race
- Having a personal residence
- Parent employed at program exit
- Availability of an automobile
- Married/Committed relationship status
- Previous CPS involvement

- Continued parental drug use
- Whether or not the child was returned home
- Program Status (graduate, early out, comparison group)

In the logistic regression model, however, the latter two variables proved to be significant predictors of subsequent CPS involvement (See Table 10.12). This logistic regression model achieved an R^2 of .502 and a critical chi square score of 37.975.

Table 10.12: Logistic Regression Model Predicting Subsequent CPS Involvement

	B (S.E.)	Exp(B)
Parent Race	-1.183 (1.158)	.306
Parent has Personal Residence	.601 (.721)	1.823
Parent Employed @ Program Exit	-.755 (.774)	.470
Family Reunifieda	3.048* (1.402)	21.067
Dependency Category 1 (< 12 months)b	-1.265 (1.661)	.282
Dependency Category 2 (13-24 months)	-3.181* (1.554)	.042
Dependency Category 3 (25-36 months)	-3.352* (1.602)	.035
Family Previously CPS-Involved	.942 (.762)	2.565
Parent Continues Drug Use	1.434 (.892)	4.196
Child Ultimately Placed with Relatives/Parents[c]	-3.318* (1.151)	.036
Program Status 1 (Comparison Group)d	-2.435* (1.239)	.088
Program Status 2 (Early Outs)	-1.183 (1.158)	.407

Table 10.12 (Continued): Logistic Regression Model Predicting Subsequent CPS Involvement

	B (S.E.)	Exp(B)
Parent Age Group 1 (20-25 years old)[e]	.601 (.721)	4.086
Parent Age Group 2 (26-30 years old)	-.755 (.774)	1.771
Parent Age Group 3 (31-35 years old)	3.048* (1.402)	1.918
Parent Married/In Committed Relationship	-1.265 (1.661)	.304
Constant	-3.181* (1.554)	16.729

Note: N = 124 *p<.05

[a] Family Reunified (0 = No; 1 = Yes)

[b] The reference category for dependency length is 37-49 months.

[c] Child ultimately placed with parents or extended family members = 1; Child ultimately placed with non-relatives = 0

[d] The reference category for program status is Graduate

[e] The reference category for parent age is ≥36 years old at program entry (or concurrent time for comparison group).

The analysis indicates that having a child returned to the home is a significant predictor of a families' subsequent involvement with CPS. Conversely, longer dependency lengths (more than 12 months), whether the child was ultimately placed with family (versus foster care), and whether the parent decided against participating in the FTC program all indicated families were less likely to have subsequent CPS involvement. This may indicate that more difficult dependency cases take longer to dismiss, involve parents less likely to engage in recovery services, and are therefore less likely to result in the return of the children to the parents, thus negating the need for further CPS involvement.

Following is a similar analysis examining predictors of continued drug use by parents.

Table 10.13: Significant Predictors of Parent Continued Drug Use

	Chi-Square	df	Uncertainty Coefficient	Cramer's V
Family Reunified	43.937*	1	.279	.600
Program Status	22.638*	1	.138	.431
Automobile Available	7.804*	1	.050	.260
Employed at Program Exit	7.714*	1	.047	.252
Parent Age	7.050	3	.043	.240
Length of Dependency	4.805	3	.035	.213
Parent Race	2.326	1	.014	.138
Personal Residence	1.467	1	.009	.110
Parent Gender	1.277	1	.008	.102
≥High School Education	1.087	1	.007	.101
Previous CPS Involvement	.253	1	.002	.046
Married/Committed Relationship	.045	1	.000	.019

Note: N = 124 *p<.05

The chi square analysis indicated that family reunification, program completion, and employment were all predictive of parents abstinence from drug use. A logistic regression analysis testing the same variables resulted in the following model.

The logistic regression model reported in Table 10.14 was statistically significant with an R^2 of .597 and a critical chi square score of 58.696. The results of the analysis indicate that dependencies that lasted twenty-four months or less were positively correlated with continued parental drug use, while family reunification was negatively correlated with parents' continued drug use. As previously discussed, the majority of dependencies lasted less than twenty-four months due to CPS' federal ASFA timeline mandates. Therefore, this correlation is likely spurious. An expected negative correlation emerged between continued parental drug use and family reunification; however this analysis did not provide new insight into the explanation of continued drug use.

Table 10.14: Logistic Regression Model Predicting Parents' Continued Drug Use

	B (S.E.)	Exp(B)
Program Status 1 (Comparison Group)	-.541 (1.041)	.582
Program Status 2 (Early Outs)	-.402 (.998)	.669
Parent Age Group 1 (20-25 years old)[a]	1.568 (.949)	4.796
Parent Age Group 2 (26-30 years old)	-.729 (1.016)	.483
Parent Age Group 3 (31-35 years old)	.822 (.949)	2.275
Parent Race (Caucasian/Non-Caucasian)	-.297 (1.024)	.743
Parent Gender	-.402 (.832)	.669
Parent has Personal Residence	.226 (.681)	1.254
Dependency Category 1 ($\leq$ 12 months)[b]	3.941* (1.672)	51.468
Dependency Category 2 (13-24 months)	2.622* (1.321)	13.759
Dependency Category 3 (25-36 months)	1.504 (1.314)	4.498
Parent has Automobile Available	-.595 (.621)	.552
Parent Employed at Program Exit	-1.237 (.690)	.290
Child placed with Relatives or Foster Care	.451 (.645)	1.569

Table 10.14 (Continued): Logistic Regression Model Predicting Parents' Continued Drug Use

	B (S.E.)	Exp(B)
Parent Married/In Committed Relationship	-.122 (.680)	.885
Family Previously CPS-Involved	-.803 (.733)	.448
Constant	1.196 (1.879)	3.306

Note: N = 124 *p<.05

[a] The reference category for parent age is ≥36 years old at program entry (or concurrent time for the comparison group).

[b] The reference category for dependency length is 37-49 months.

Couples in the Program

While not a statistically significant indicator, relationships appeared to be a good gauge of how a client would fare in the FTC program. Post-program interviews revealed that clients who were able to cut off old ties with drug using friends and partners tended to do better in the program, (and post-program) than clients who insisted on maintaining established relationships with their using associates. Although officially the government cannot regulate client behavior with respect to this issue, FTC clients were routinely required to choose between their partner and their children, unless both parents were participating in the program. CWS workers' standard response was, "You're right, we can't tell you who to be friends with. We can, however, decline to return your children if we feel the environment you provide for them is unsafe." If both parents were participating in the FTC program, predominantly both of the parents involved proceeded, or regressed, together in the program.

Twenty-two couples were part of this study population. Table 10.15 sets forth findings which depict each couple's status in relation to their participation in the FTC program.

As depicted in Table 10.15, in nearly one-third of the couples, *both* successfully completed the program. In approximately one-fourth of the couples, only one of the partners completed the program, while another quarter of the couples were either discharged or opted out prematurely from the program. Also of note – the minority of couples in this study were married.

Table 10.15: Program Status of Couples in the Study Population

	Couples (n=22)	% Married
One Graduated*	6	33%
One Opted Out	1	0%
Both Graduated	7	43%
Both Discharged	4	25%
Both Opted Out	2	0%
Both Did not Opt In	2	50%

*For the 6 couples where only 1 partner graduated: 3 of the non-graduating partners were discharged; 1 opted out of FTC; 1 never entered the program; and, 1 became incarcerated. This individual was not included in other measures in this study.

Family Treatment Court: A Turning Point in the Life Course

The findings from this research were somewhat mixed regarding support for Sampson and Laub's (2003) life course theory. Their assertion that institutional or structural *turning points* can provide a new situation that: 1) "knives off" the past from the present; 2) provides both supervision and monitoring as well as new opportunities of social support and growth; 3) change in and productive structure of routine activities, and; 4) provides the opportunity for identity transformation (148) found some application in this family treatment court.

Although replacing drug-dependent relationships with sober ones helped create success in completing the FTC program and in reunifying parents with children, this research did not find support for Sampson and Laub's assertion that "Strong attachment to a spouse (or cohabitant) combined with close emotional ties creates a social bond or interdependence between two individuals that, all else being equal, should lead to a reduction in deviant behavior" (Sampson & Laub, 1993, p. 140). This can be attributed to several factors. First, the majority (70%) of study subjects in this research were female as opposed to the exclusively male cohort found in Sampson and Laub's studies on which their Life Course Theory is based. Second, as discussed by Sampson and Laub, the "drug of choice" for their cohort was alcohol, as "drugs like cocaine and heroin were not pervasive" at the time (1993, p. 254). While alcohol abuse is strongly associated with crime and wreaks devastation on families, alcohol is distinctly different from contemporary drugs in two important ways: 1) Alcohol is a legal substance, and; 2) Alcohol is a depressant, as opposed to the stimulant drugs (e.g., methamphetamine, cocaine) so prevalent today. Stimulants increase alertness, attention, and energy, as well as elevate blood pressure and increase heart rate and respiration (National Institute on Drug Abuse, 2005), whereas alcohol causes decreased coordination and attention, impaired concentration and reaction time, drowsiness, memory problems, and mood changes ("Module 5," 2006). Further, today's drug users have a wider array of substances to choose from which only intensifies the experience and duration of addiction.

This research more accurately supported the arguments of Simons, Stewart, Gordon, Conger & Elder (2002), who assert that association with offenders is diminished only if one's romantic partner is committed to a conventional lifestyle. Living with a partner who engages in unlawful behavior actually enhances the probability of crime for men and women, and these romantic relationships appear to exert a greater negative influence on women. The FTC treatment team frequently discussed the romantic lives of female clients and made treatment decisions based on those romantic relationships. Male clients were much less likely to have their relationships dissected during a treatment team meeting. In part, this was due to the fact that several of the male clients were in the FTC program with the mother of their children whereas most of the mothers were in the program, and parenting, without a partner. This common circumstance made the family treatment court's capacity to "provide the opportunity for identity transformation" as Sampson and Laub (2003) stress, an important aspect of the program. The FTC program's ability to help clients transform their identity from that of drug abuser to parent stemmed from the development of social capital in conventional institutions.

The Family Treatment Court as an Agent of Social Capital

The social capital phenomenon was a recurring theme witnessed throughout this research. Through courtroom observations as well as interviews with treatment team members and clients, it was clear that a client's willingness and ability to withdraw their social investment from the drug-related people, places, and things they had known most of their lives, and invest their personal energy into learning parenting skills, pursuing educational or employment endeavors in mainstream institutions, and (most difficult of all) building sober personal relationships had everything to do with their success during and after their participation in the program. The likelihood of having their family reunited and regaining the opportunity to parent their children was directly connected with their ability to build a new, healthy version of social capital.

Consistently during the two-year courtroom observations clients proved highly focused on the "genuineness" of the treatment team member's interest in them (i.e., if team members showed some social investment in them.) The vast majority of in-court complaints by clients centered around being made to feel unimportant, unheard, or ignored by members of the treatment team or by outside service providers. It was remarkable to see how, over time, clients came to feel comfortable enough to bring their concerns directly to the judge, even after having the opportunity to tell their chemical dependency counselor, their CWS worker, and their public defender. It was apparent that clients valued this direct connection to someone in such a high position of authority, someone who would genuinely listen to their worries and fears. This aspect of the relationship also served both the clients and the judge well when clients were sanctioned for program noncompliance. Feeling that the judge made a sincere investment in the client during compliant times made clients feel that the judge was making an informed decision when meting out sanctions for program noncompliance. The judge clearly knew their "whole story," and could take a more fully informed perspective into consideration when ruling on a sanction.

This investment in social capital also proved significant in relationships observed among clients of the FTC. Those who were determined to get clean from drugs latched on to the few others who also came into the program ready to sober up. Those who wanted to "play" the system to get their kids back continued to use drugs with each other during their personal time, and schooled each other in the latest methods used to adulterate a positive UA. One treatment counselor explained such behavior:

> Clients don't want to be here at first, but then they begin to take ownership of the program. They call each other's BS. They begin to think, "This is MY program and you (relapsers) are not going to mess it up." Those who are working the program get really pissed off with those who try to skate through. Some even become afraid to function without the support of the program.

While some clients chose from the beginning which path they were going to take, others entered the program with a mindset that transitioned from "going through the motions," to achieving recovery. For a number of clients, after some clean time and sincere social investment by other clients and team members into their sobriety, they developed a genuine desire to stay sober and reunite their family. Unfortunately, some clients were unable to make this change. Some who came into the program convinced they were ready to get clean found the program too rigorous for their mettle, or realized through engagement in the program that they were not ready to give up drugs and needed to make permanent, alternate arrangements for their children.

The courtroom atmosphere was also distinctly affected by the cohesiveness of the client group. As clients filed into the courtroom, they knew who had just been "counseled" by the public defender and therefore receiving a sanction that day. If the group was emotionally invested in one another, there was a lot of tension in the air. As the judge handed down the team-recommended sanction, other clients would shake their heads, tear-up, even openly cry. If the group members were not emotionally close, the gallery only stared on with disinterest as one of their cohorts received his or her sanction. The same was true for client rewards; if the group was close, the gallery erupted in applause and cheers when one of their own was acknowledged. If not cohesive, the group would respond with forced, scattered applause at the judge's beckoning. Some members of the gallery even look at each other and sneer in jealousy as one of their group received accolades.

The courtroom atmosphere also changes with the absence or presence of children. Although clients are discouraged from bringing their children to court, team members easily adapted to the presence of children in the courtroom. At counsel table, the AAGs checked behind their chairs for toddlers before pushing back to stand and address the court. They would even toss a wayward toy back to its rightful owner without missing a professional beat. Defense attorneys would present children at counsel table with cups of water to occupy them so their parents could more easily concentrate on the proceedings. Team members raised their voices when addressing the court in order to be heard over an exploring child banging the courtroom mini-blinds at the window next to the judge's bench. At times, the children's presence in the courtroom served as extraordinary reminders of what was at stake for parents in the program. Clients and team members alike celebrated the birth of a healthy, drug-free baby, or conversely, watched somberly, almost in horror, as the judge asked clients who have habitually relapsed to bring their child to the bench and return to counsel table. All are fixated as the judge tells these parents that the baby she is holding is the one being hurt by their choices, and they have one last chance to have their child returned to them, to provide proper care, or the next time they will be handing the child back to the judge will be their last.

Family Planning

Because of the 'family' aspect of family treatment court, both clients and treatment team members were asked about the issue of family planning as part of the program. Child welfare workers said they were prohibited by policy to discuss birth control or family planning with clients. Conversely, when one walks into the treatment team's office, there is a basket of condoms on the front counter and pamphlets advertising a multitude of free, state-provided contraception displayed in the waiting area. The treatment counselors reported talking with clients about family planning during treatment sessions. However, when FTC graduates were asked if they remembered talking about family planning or birth control during their time in the program; all replied, "no."

Some of the women graduates recalled a discussion by their treatment counselor about the option of masturbation as opposed to indiscriminate sex with male partners. Clients characterized these discussions as "gross," "embarrassing" and "not helpful." Further, when asked if the FTC program changed the way they thought about birth control or family planning, graduates again uniformly replied "no." Many of the women in the program reported having tubal ligation surgery. Several reported being abstinent – some because their partners were incarcerated, others stated that a sexual relationship was so far down on their list of priorities that they had not thought about birth control for some time. A few male and female clients reported using condoms, and many of the men reported that their partners were on the pill or had undergone a tubal ligation. Some graduates reported not using any form of birth control.

Findings Related to Research Hypotheses

The following section provides answers based on this research findings to the hypotheses posed in this research.

H1: Clients who participate in the family treatment court have a higher family reunification rate than non-participants.

As indicated above, program graduates were reunified with their children at much greater rates (86%) than the comparison groups. Only 25% of opt outs, 22% of the comparison group, and 11% of discharged individuals had their children returned to them.

H2: Clients who participate in the family treatment court are re-referred to CPS less frequently than non-participants, once their FTC dependency is dismissed.

While FTC graduates were reunified with their children at much higher rates than non-graduates or the comparison group, their subsequent CPS involvement was either comparable or higher to the other groups, as depicted in Table 10.16. It is worth noting, however, that 90% of discharged clients and 67% of the comparison group were subsequently CPS-involved due to the birth of successive children, whereas only 15% of subsequent CPS involvement for program graduates was due to having more children. Also of note is the finding that 23% (6) of the graduates versus 4% (1) of the comparison group parents who were subsequently CPS-involved did not have their children removed on the subsequent episode.

Table 10.16: Subsequent CPS-Involvement by Program Status

Program Status	Subsequent CPS Involvement	% New Children
Graduates	50%	15%
(33 of 44)[a]	(13/26)	(2/13)
Discharges	38%	90%
(21 of 28)[a]	(10/26)	(9/10)
Opt Outs (12 of 16)[a]	---*	---*
Comparison Group	12%	67%
(25 of 36)[a]	(3/26)	(2/3)

*None of the clients who opted out of the program were reunited with their children.

[a] Eleven graduates, 7 discharged clients, 4 clients who opted out, and 11 individuals in the comparison group began their process in 2005, and had not been involved with CPS through 2006 (when CPS records were pulled).

H3: Clients who participate in the family treatment court remain clean and sober for longer periods than non-participants.

This hypothesis was difficult to assess due to the comparison, discharged and opt out groups largely not being monitored for their drug use. The majority of these individuals (75% or more) did not engage in any type of treatment as required by CPS and were therefore not reunited with their children.

H4: Clients who participate in the family treatment court retain stable employment for longer periods than non-participants.

While the percentage of employed graduates was higher than any other group (both pre- and post-program, see Table 10.17), the FTC program did not offer any special assistance in this regard. As previously reported, the program discouraged employment during Phase I – the first 18 weeks of treatment. Therefore, any employment data is client-driven.

Table 10.17: Employment Rate by Program Status

	Graduates	Discharged	Opt Outs	Did Not Opt In
Pre-Program Employment	20% (9)	14% (4)	13% (2)	3% (1)
Post-Program Employment	41% (18)	14% (4)	25% (4)	28% (10)

H5: Clients who participate in the family treatment court establish permanent housing for longer periods than non-participants.

Table 10.18: Housing Attainment by Program Status

	Graduates	Discharged	Opt Outs	Did Not Opt In
Personal Residence Pre-Program	73% (32)	68% (19)	56% (9)	39% (14)
Personal Residence Post-Program	91% (40)	39% (11)	56% (9)	42% (15)

The research did provide empirical support for this hypothesis. Because stable housing is a CWS-imposed condition for family reunification, the post-program housing rates for graduates was much higher than for the other groups. As with employment, the FTC program referred clients to housing programs but did not directly assist clients with this service. However, several clients who graduated during the first half of the study period reported in interviews that their FTC CWS worker helped them move to the top of the subsidized housing list. Subsequent graduates did not report this occurrence.

H6: Clients who participate in the family treatment court attain higher education levels than non-participants.

FTC clients were so busy meeting the demands of this intense program that none of them engaged in educational endeavors while in the program. Only a small number of graduates (6/44) enrolled in an educational program after leaving the program.

CHAPTER 11

Family Treatment Court Program Issues

Recruitment

One challenge that the FTC constantly faced was recruiting and enrolling a full slate of clients into the program. This was consistently a point of concern that emerged through treatment team interviews. An FTC treatment counselor noted:

> It's hard to make clients understand that a year-long program is exactly what they need. It's scary to people.

One of the public defenders elaborated:

> In the beginning [of a dependency], everyone thinks they can get clean in three months on their own. When there are allegations of substance abuse, the court wants clean UAs. Clients think they can provide that on their own. I sometimes argue to clients that [the FTC treatment provider] has more money and mental health resources than other programs."
>
> It's hard to convince clients to admit they have a substance abuse problem anyway. They don't realize they have a problem. You can't get clean unless you admit you've got a problem. We [public defenders] have to tell potential clients (about the FTC program), "It's a ton more work." We are very candid with

> clients about the rigorousness of FTC. We tell the clients they can't do anything else while they're in the FTC program because it is so intensive, and requires the bulk of their time. We have to be abstract about who, and how many people will help the client, and in what ways. We can't make any promises to clients (e.g., "You'll get your kids back sooner.")

One CWS worker identified the struggle for the program:

> Low enrollment numbers. We are selling treatment court wrong. Clients are told, "You'll get your kids back quicker." The sell should be, "You're going to get into treatment sooner and have a real chance to get clean with these intensive services."

In the early stages of the program, team members did tell parents and other referring agencies that FTC clients would get their kids back sooner than other parents. One child welfare worker explained:

> We advertised FTC as a way for clients to get their kids back faster. That's not true. I've had non-FTC clients who get their kids back faster. We do clients a disservice in telling them that.

Based on team members' experience with the customary dependency system, this seemed a logical conclusion to draw when the program began. Clients entered treatment at least two months faster with the FTC program, and they had the support of a multi-agency team that was held accountable in court twice a month. In reality, however, children were not generally returned sooner to FTC clients due in large part to the increased oversight of the court and regular, frequent information sharing among agencies that shone a bright light on any concerns team members had with the parents. Having to back away from this statement made recruitment into the program even more difficult.

A public defender explained:

> Because we can no longer return their kids earlier, there's no carrot. There's no benefit.

In the first two years of the program, treatment team members scheduled program presentations with the public defender's office, the attorney general's office, and the CPS office in order to enhance referrals. Frequently, however, referrals from other agencies came too late – seven months or more into the dependency. In the second year, the treatment counselors began attending dependency hearings with the intention of informing potential clients about the program on the spot, rather than depending on the client to call the program to schedule an appointment. Not one person was recruited into the program using this approach.

In addition to obstacles with initial recruitment, the program experienced substantial attrition rates typically associated with substance abuse treatment. Published research suggests that approximately one-half to two-thirds of individuals who schedule an initial intake appointment for drug abuse treatment fail to show up for their first intake session. Festinger, Lamb, Kountz, Kirby, & Marlowe (1995) found 58% of clients failed to show for initial intake appointment for cocaine treatment (p. 111). Festinger, Lamb, Kirby, & Marlowe (1996) found 67% of clients failed to show for standard intake appointment for cocaine treatment and 41% of clients offered immediate intake appointment failed to show (p. 387). Festinger, Lamb, Marlowe, & Kirby (2002) found 52% of clients failed to show for intake appointment for cocaine treatment, and 28% of clients offered immediate intake appointment failed to show (p. 135).

Of those who do attend an initial intake, between 40% and 80% drop out of treatment within one to three months, and 80% to 90% drop out within a year (See Gainy, Wells, Hawkins, & Catalano, 1993). Stark (1992) concluded that the majority of programs report over 50% attrition within the first month of drug abuse treatment, 52% to 75% attrition in outpatient alcoholism treatment by the fourth session, and 80% attrition for heroin addicts by fourth session of drug-free treatment (p. 94). Simpson, Joe, & Brown, (1997) found that nationally 42% of clients drop out of treatment within 90 days (p. 300). Satel (1999) concluded that 80% to 90% of addicts leave treatment by the end of the first year and "Among such dropouts, relapse within a year is the rule" (p. 2). Research also suggests that three months of substance abuse treatment may be the minimum threshold for detecting dose-response effects for the interventions, and twelve months may be the minimum threshold for observing meaningful reductions in drug use. Simpson, et al. (1997) found that in a nationally representative sample of drug abuse treatment programs, clients remaining in treatment three months or longer had better outcomes in all areas of functioning, and clients who stayed one year or longer had significantly greater reductions in drug use. Given these statistics, the FTC program did well to retain 60% (53 of 88) clients in treatment for more than nine months and to graduate half of all clients who entered this intensive, year-long program.

In addition to recruitment difficulties, the FTC program struggled with appropriate referrals. One child welfare worker observed:

> In reality, we haven't been doing a good job of screening. The AGs check the legal record to see how long the family has been in the [CPS] system (to make sure they meet program time requirements).

A public defender noted:

> Some clients should not have been let into the program. When mental health issues are involved, clients leave the program fairly quickly. For example, one client did well in treatment, but couldn't address parenting issues. It is difficult to tell about those cases up front.

One of the GALs added:

> We had some bad fits as far as people coming into the program who weren't very motivated or weren't properly educated about the program.

To improve the process, the child welfare supervisor began reviewing CPS petitions for dependency to screen for possible FTC clients, then e-mailed the CPS unit to ask them if certain cases would fit well in FTC, asking, "In your opinion, does this mother have a realistic chance of getting her kids back? Is she amenable to treatment?"

One population subset that turned out a poor match for the FTC program were developmentally disabled (DD) clients. A considerable amount of time was spent during team meetings trying to figure out how to help DD parents succeed in the program, and discussing whether DD clients should be held to the same standard as other clients. McGee, et al. (2000) observe in this respect, "The drug court program does not work very well for persons with serious (so-called dual diagnosed) mental or emotional health problems who cannot function in regular group settings. Special "tracks" may need to be created for persons who are seriously mentally impaired and who will not be able to keep up with the fast-paced case plans developed for the "typical" family drug court participant which require insight and far-sight" (p. 49).

Developmentally disabled clients frequently served as a point of contention between treatment counselors and child welfare workers. While the client could stay clean for extended periods of time, their capacity to make or manage money, run a household, or consistently care for their children in an age-appropriate manner was often insufficient. Treatment would argue that the DD client was succeeding in the program because he or she was staying clean and attending all of their treatment meetings. CWS would acknowledge the client's treatment compliance, but point out that during supervised visitations or hands-on parenting classes with their children, the client was not able to meet the most basic needs of their children (e.g., healthy/appropriate food choices; age-appropriate play or sleep needs; discipline.) CWS felt it important to observe these parents for extended periods in a visitation setting to assess their parenting abilities, while the treatment counselors and public defenders pushed to have the children returned to the now sober parent. In a change of roles, CWS would argue that the increased frustration level experienced by parents could serve as a trigger for relapse (treatment's purview), while treatment asserted that the sooner the children were returned, the longer the parent would have program support while experiencing the challenges of family rebuilding (CWS's purview). One guardian ad litem noted the following:

> While some parents are able to stay clean and sober, sometimes because of their disabilities they aren't able to parent. They have other issues (besides drug use) that get in the way of parenting.

Several developmentally disabled clients successfully graduated the program without ever having their children returned to them.

As previously discussed in the Co-occurring Disorders section of Chapter 5, the FTC program was not adequately set up to address the needs of clients with mental health problems. The inadequate provision of services begins with the lack of routine assessments of potential clients. Due to the high cost of psychological evaluations, FTC clients were only assessed for co-occurring disorders if they struggled inexplicably in treatment, or if they were persistent in their desire to be assessed. Some clients were discharged from the program after several months with a recommendation of a psychological evaluation, never having had one while in the program. A therapeutic jurisprudence approach would seem to demand a psychological evaluation be conducted at program *entry* in order for the court to best accomplish its restorative objective. However, one AAG accurately concludes, "*Psychological evaluations are not any good until clients are clean.*"

Unfortunately, even if issues other than substance abuse were identified as contributing to a client's relapse, the team possessed rather few resources to assist them in this regard. When the on-site mental health counselor retired six months into the observation period as his funding expired, he was never replaced. In an interview he noted:

> All of the FTC counselors have mental health backgrounds but lack the clinical expertise . . . They could provide the six to eight mental health sessions to FTC clients . . .They needed clinical supervision, but that was never sorted out.

If a client had a high-needs child, however, there was an abundance of services available for the child. One child warranted seven specialists while the mother struggled in treatment. Services for drug-affected families are largely child-focused (service providers helping the child) rather than family-focused (i.e., help the parent through training and practice in self-sufficiency to raise the child). During a team discussion of a particularly difficult case where the program client continued to relapse, one of the defense attorneys observed the following:

> I think we've been working on chemical dependency for a long time and it doesn't seem to be working. Does (client)

> need mental health counseling? Every once in a while childhood traumas come up (in treatment) and I don't know about it. I never asked [the client] about childhood issues because things were going so well (in treatment).

In another team meeting, the public defender observed that perhaps the team "brushed personality disorders under the rug" because it is more difficult to deal with and focus on than substance abuse. Even treatment team members fell into the trap of believing if a client can sustain long periods of sobriety and parenting, they can get by without any mental health services and just 'work' their way to good mental health.

Relapse During Program Participation

This section discusses relapse and missed UAs by program participants while in the program. Missed UAs are included as they are viewed by treatment providers as an indicator of drug use by clients. This is followed by a discussion of missed treatment meetings by clients.

Table 11.1: Relapse/Missed UA Comparison for FTC Participants

	Relapse		**Missed UA**	
Violation	**Graduate (n=37)***	**Early Out (n=35)****	**Graduate (n=37)**	**Early Out (n=35)**
1	7	7	14	13
2	5	9	10	9
3	9	9	3	7
4	6	4	3	9
5	5	3	0	8
6	1	1	4	4
7	2	1	2	2
8	2	1	0	3
9	1	0	1	1
10	0	0	0	1
Total	**38**	**35**	**37**	**57**

*The total graduates in this table of 37 excludes 7 of the 44 program graduates who completed the program without committing any program violations.

** The total early outs of 35 excludes 8 of the 44 early outs who were in the program for 2 weeks or less and one early out client who was in the program for 14 weeks, but for whom no treatment court report records could be located.

Note that while the graduate and early out groups are similar in the total number of program-identified relapses, the early out group missed a substantially greater number of UAs than did the graduate group. This could indicate that while graduates may have used at similar rates as the early out group while in the program, they were more inclined to continue their regular participation in the program, including attending their scheduled UAs, and accept the consequences of their use. Early outs appeared more likely to disengage from the program as they continued their drug use. This is also illustrated in the following table:

Table 11.2: Average Relapse/Missed UA by FTC Participants

	Relapse	**Missed UA**
Graduates (n=37)*	1.03	.97
Early Outs (n=35)*	1.00	1.63

*7 FTC graduates completed the program without a dirty or missed UA. Nine of the early outs left the program prior to relapse detection.

On several occasions, team members would comment on the seemingly generous number of excused absences granted to clients by their treatment provider. As a rule, if clients missed treatment group meetings, one-on-one counseling sessions with their treatment counselor, or community support meetings, they were given an unsatisfactory report and sanctioned for program non-compliance. However, if clients convinced their treatment counselor they had a good reason for missing treatment meetings, the counselor could "excuse" them from attending their full schedule of required treatment commitments. In effect, this removed the treatment team from inclusive oversight of program clients. On average, women clients were granted 18 excused absences during their time in the program, men averaged 14 excused absences. As illustrated in Table 11.3, clients who eventually opted out of the program were granted a considerably higher rate of excused absences as compared to clients who were ultimately discharged or graduated from the program. This finding is in line with the AAG's observation in Chapter 9, of clients wanting to be held accountable while in the program.

Table 11.3: Treatment Excused Absences and No Shows

	Average Excused Absences	Excused Absences	No Shows
Graduates (44)	12	4%	2%
Discharges (24)	10	6%	15%
Opt Outs (12)	16	13%	9%

Sanctions

Freeman-Wilson (2003) summarizes the legal status of sanctions related to addiction:

> More than 40 years ago, in Robinson v. State of California (370 U.S. 660, 666 (1962)), the U.S. Supreme Court invalidated a California statute that criminalized the "status" of narcotics addiction on Eighth Amendment grounds. The Robinson court concluded, however, that, "a State might establish a program of compulsory treatment for those addicted to narcotics" and that "penal sanctions might be imposed for failure to comply with established compulsory treatment procedures" (665).

The Supreme Court's decision opened the door to drug treatment programs that included the use of penal sanctions, but also recognized that drug addiction is an "illness which may be contracted innocently or involuntarily" (370 U.S. at 667).

Although the FTC public defenders eventually agreed to jail as part of the graduated sanctions for program clients, they continued to assert the position that jail is a "criminal sanction" and that "FTC was not a criminal court." However, state statutes permit the issuance of jail time of up to seven days for civil contempt for failing to follow a court order (See RCW 13.34.165). This is the statute the AAGs used to request jail time for clients who habitually relapsed or disengaged from treatment.

Other family treatment courts have chosen not to include jail time as a high-level sanction for clients struggling with program compliance sober (Edwards & Ray, 2005, p. 5).

As stated in the FTC Program Description, when clients opted to take part in the program, they signed a Treatment Agreement that included a list of the program sanctions. The graduated sanctions are as follows:

- Verbal reprimand by the court
- Jury Box (clients are required to attend a Felony Drug Court session to observe people who may be further along on their addiction path and more deeply involved in the criminal justice system.)
- Client may be held back from progressing to the next level (phase) of treatment
- More intensive treatment required (e.g., inpatient)
- More frequent UA/BAs
- Community Service
- Loss of unsupervised visits with children
- Up to 5 days in jail (court order for 7 days resulted in serving 5 days good time)
- Termination from Family Treatment Court and returned to Dependency Court
- Child removed from parent's home to protect the safety of the child

Each additional program violation was to result in the next level of sanction; however, this was not routinely the case.

Halfway through the observation period the team decided to more closely match the severity of the sanction with what they perceived to be the severity of the program violation. Team discussions centered around the inequity of, for example, a jury box sanction for both a client who committed the minor infraction of turning in their meeting slips late, versus a client who relapsed. Tables comparing sanction severity both before and after implementation of the new sanction policy follows:

Table 11.4: Adherence to Graduated Sanctions 2003-2004

	Graduated Sanction (67)	Less Harsh than Graduated Sanction (42)	More Harsh Than Graduated Sanction (47)
1st Sanction	43%	--	26%
2nd Sanction	12%	21%	43%
3rd Sanction	21%	17%	17%
4th Sanction	12%	14%	11%
5th Sanction	1.5%	17%	4%
6th Sanction	6%	12%	--
7th Sanction	--	14%	--
8th Sanction	--	5%	--
9th Sanction	3%	--	--
10th Sanction	1.5%	--	--

Table 11.5: Customized Sanctions 2005-2006

	Graduated Sanction (55)	Less Harsh than Graduated Sanction (37)	More Harsh Than Graduated Sanction (30)
1st Sanction	38%	--	27%
2nd Sanction	16%	8%	33%
3rd Sanction	13%	11%	20%
4th Sanction	2%	24%	17%
5th Sanction	11%	19%	3%
6th Sanction	6%	16%	--
7th Sanction	2%	16%	--
8th Sanction	9%	3%	--
9th Sanction	4%	3%	--

For 2003-2004, there were a total of 156 program violations. Note that less than half (43%) of sanctions fell into the graduated sanctions schedule in 2003 – 2004. Thirty percent were more harsh (the majority of those occurring after the first or second program violation), and 27% of sanctions were less harsh than the graduated schedule. Of the total

156 sanctions imposed in 2003 and 2004, 22 (14%) were suspended, and another 10 (6%) were not imposed due to the client exiting the program, or the team combining later sanctions with the preceding one (See Table 11.6).

For 2005-2006, program violations totaled 122. Although the team decided to deviate from the graduated sanctions schedule with the intention of customizing the sanction to the severity of the program violation, the distribution of the harshness of penalties imposed by the team was remarkably similar to the outcomes prior to the deviation. Forty-five percent of sanctions followed the graduated sanctions schedule, 25% were more harsh than the graduated sanctions schedule, and 30% were less harsh. Of the total 122 sanctions imposed in 2005 and 2006, 24 (20%) were suspended, and another 9 (7%) were not imposed (See Table 11.6). Note that during both time frames sanctions tended to move from more harsh to less harsh than the graduated schedule as the number of program violations increased.

These data support the assertion held by team members – clients are given several chances to stay in and successfully complete the program. The data also indicate that in practice, the policy change did not result in a substantially different sanctioning schedule.

Table 11.6: Comparison of Sanction Adherence

	Graduated Sanction	Less Harsh	More Harsh	Sanction Suspended	Sanction Not Imposed
2003-2004	43%	27%	30%	14%	6%
2005-2006	45%	30%	25%	20%	7%

While the intended policy change of sanction severity did not materialize, over the course of the team evaluation, all of the team members became more proficient in examining the long-term effects of a particular sanction on a family and more willing to deviate from the graduated sanction scale for what they perceived to be the actions taken in benefit of the client. For example, instead of customarily sending a mother who has custody of her children to jail for a fourth sanction (not relapse), and disrupting the children with a temporary placement while the mother served her sentence, the team might determine that an essay on the relevance of program compliance to permanent family reunification would be more appropriate. On several occasions, the team opted not to send clients who were taking mental health prescriptions to jail because they would have to go several days without their critical medications as the jail could not administer them without a lengthy approval process.

Sanctions were the most oft-cited topic of discussion at the monthly team process meetings. In the fourth month of the team observation, the AAG noted that the program had deviated from immediate imposition of sanctions, and instead,

> [When a] sanctionable event occurs we allow the team time to research why the sanctionable event happened. Why don't we deal with it right then? Why do we need to delay the sanction for days while we investigate the excuse? The team addresses it 2-3 weeks later, when the team has lost interest. The sanction feels meaningless.

The treatment counselors agreed that one of the main benefits of treatment court is the immediacy of support and sanctions for clients who are struggling in the program. Initially, the public defender expressed a concern about giving up the right to advocate for the clients; however, ultimately the public defender agreed with the importance of program predictability and consistent follow-through.

In a survey conducted by the American University Drug Court Clearinghouse and Technical Assistance Project in 1997, 82% of drug court participants reported that the possibility of sanctions being imposed for non-compliance with the program requirements was a very important distinction between drug court and prior treatment programs. Harrell (2000) found drug court program participants in the sanctions track often feeling that, "Agreeing in advance to the sanctions and the rules for applying penalties gave them a feeling of control." When a jail sanction was imposed on an FTC client, more often than not the client was allowed to appear for booking on their own, by a specified date and time. If clients were openly rebellious to the program, the team would sometimes request that the judge order the client taken into custody during court and escorted by law enforcement to the adjacent jail as a salient example to the group. While scheduling on-demand deputy transport was often difficult, the walk-in custody procedure was fraught with problems. Numerous times when clients arrived in booking to serve their jail sentence they were turned away because the jail did not have the proper paperwork – even if the client had their own documentation with them. The AAGs and even the judge had to initiate several communications with the jail to rectify the situation. Even when the court faxed over the paperwork as requested by the jail, some turn-aways continued to take place for months thereafter.

Program Evolution

Originally, the FTC program was set up with three treatment phases of eighteen weeks each. Late in the observation period, the team discussed adding a fourth phase for aftercare, as many clients seemed to need more time to establish themselves outside the program. One of the most oft-cited resources for a sober support system is Narcotics Anonymous. Narcotics Anonymous (NA), and its precursor Alcoholics Anonymous (AA), are often a part of the treatment protocol assigned to drug court participants (Gallas, 2004). While the program model is widely recognized and broadly regarded as successful, a substantial group of individuals exists that dislikes the 12-Step model for a number of reasons, including the religious content. White (1998) listed some frequent criticisms of the 12-Step approach, including the complaints that the model only treats symptoms rather than the underlying cause of addiction; that the programs tend to disempower participants; that the program ignores environmental factors such as socio-economic status; and that the religious language and concepts keep many addicts from wanting to become affiliated with a 12-Step program (p. 156). The FTC treatment provider received a change in mandate early in 2005 allowing them to legally refer clients to, and talk about, AA and NA even though they are religious-based programs.

FTC graduates' experience with NA meetings were rather negative. Representative comments from graduates included:

> You can't mention Jesus in those meetings.
>
> I enjoyed treatment, but after FTC I quit going to self-help groups. People were talking about explicit drug acts – the exact thing I was trying to get over.

> I stopped going to AA/NA meetings. They aren't that helpful right now.
>
> I don't like self-help meetings. They're a bunch of cry babies. I'm not attending any self-help groups. Three years of treatment is enough for me.
>
> Self-help groups like AA or NA are brainwashing cults. They say if you use again you'll either end up dead, in a mental institution, or in jail. Also the sponsors have favorites.

However, like the treatment team, graduates of the program also saw the need for a fourth phase of treatment to give them additional time to make their transition into sober social circles. Clients felt like imposters in the midst of what they perceived to be people completely different from them – sober.

> We had all these friends, then we stopped doing drugs and we had **nobody**. You have to cut your losses. We could either keep our friends or keep our [child]. I feel guilt. I can't endanger my family to have a friendship that isn't real in the first place. On the news, we saw a meth house burn and I know the victims, but I can't reach out to them because it threatens my sobriety and my family. We're still kind of loners. We haven't met new people. Through work we've started to be invited to barbeques.
>
> Childcare is difficult. Old friends use so they can't help. My new, sober friends all work.
>
> Giving up my (using) friends was the hard part for me. Giving up everything I knew for what I didn't know. It was different. We're just now learning to accept people being nice.

Another evolution in the program was the addition of a men-only treatment group. Approximately one year after the program began one of the male treatment counselors developed a group exclusive to men in order to provide an opportunity for fathers to discuss issues unique to them. Also, in an effort to try to accommodate employed program clients, evening groups were added to the existing day treatment groups; however, any client could choose to attend evening rather than morning group treatment sessions if they wished. Several FTC graduates felt this was a weakness of the program. During a post-graduation interview one former client stated:

> They (FTC) should not have changed the program to where you could attend either day or night sessions. Letting the new clients go to night sessions was a BIG mistake. I think clients need to go to day sessions for the first 90 days they're in the program. The hardest thing is changing your schedule.

One of the FTC treatment counselors spoke of the importance of holding boundaries with the clients, and giving them structure.

> We learned it was a mistake to allow unemployed clients to go to night group sessions. Our graduates told us, "You don't let people sleep until they want to get up and go to treatment."

As a result, the treatment team added provisions to the program contract stating that clients must either work or volunteer on a part-time basis during the latter phases of the program. This was also intended to assist clients with resume'-building, work experience, and matching their schedules with their children's school schedules. To increase personal accountability, the program added Moral Reconation Therapy (MRT)[25] as a *requirement*, rather than elective element of the program.

Graduates also commented on the need for the program to conduct urine analysis (UA) on clients more frequently, and to be more vigilant in detecting adulterated UAs.

> One of the biggest things (drawbacks) in the program is no UAs on weekends or holidays – for instance, when New Year's Eve is on a Friday. They should have mid-weekend, or 4th of July UAs for clients. A lot more UAs are needed.

---

[25] The cognitive-behavioral treatment approach that teaches clients moral decision-making processes.

> Treatment needs to UA on Saturdays. They need a better system to UA every other day, either Monday/Wednesday/Friday or Tuesday/Thursday/Saturday.

During the observation period, at least three clients who were near graduation were finally caught after several months of adulterating their urine specimens. One male client used a fake bladder, stored under his arm, with a tube running down his side to provide a clean UA. Another client used a neighbor boy's urine in a travel-size alcohol bottle to provide clean UAs. She would cover the bottle with tin foil and insert it, upside-down, inside herself, then pierce the tin foil with her fingernail when she provided her specimen to the treatment providers. The third client used a mixture of vinegar and pickle juice prior to providing a specimen to neutralize the elevated ph levels (alkaline and acidity) in her urine due to methamphetamine use. Each of the three program participants left the program unsuccessfully just prior to their expected graduation dates. Other program clients were dismayed but not surprised by the dirty UAs and subsequent program departures. One graduate observed:

> Treatment misses a lot of relapse. There's a lot of drinking that goes on while clients are in recovery. Treatment uses guilt more than anything for clients who relapse, but if someone isn't close to the group, guilt isn't going to work.

Treatment counselors, however, were quite distraught over these departures. They examined their procedures and discussed the possibility of using specimen hats instead of cups to facilitate urine collection, allowing clients' hands to remain visible at all times while providing their specimen, and having clients lift up their shirts to the chest and turning full circle prior to providing a specimen so treatment could check them for adulterating paraphernalia. The program manager cited the increased cost of using specimen hats over cups, and concluded that all clients would eventually get tired of performing the extra work required to adulterate their specimens and get caught using. This seems a peculiar position to take, particularly for parents who have children in their care. In addition, a lot of blame was placed on the other clients who knew about the use but did not report it to program treatment counselors. To help rectify the problem, counselors affixed several mirrored squares behind the toilet, as well as on the wall opposite of where the counselor stood to supervise the UAs to better observe any suspicious behavior taking place.

Through the monthly process meetings, the team decided to change their protocol for imposing sanctions from that of waiting until the client's next regularly scheduled court date to requiring non-compliant clients to appear at the very next court date, whether or not it was their regular bi-weekly or monthly date. This was done in order to help clients re-engage in treatment more quickly, supported by the influence of the judge. As previously discussed in the sanctions section of this research, the FTC program was set up with a graduated sanctions format. Beginning in early 2005, the team began to shuffle graduated sanctions to better fit the severity of the program violation. For example, a second program violation is usually sanctioned with five hours of community service. However, if a client's second violation was leaving inpatient treatment against medical advice (AMA), the team would discuss which sanction they felt would best help the client get back on track, which could include some jail time. The team increased the swiftness and severity of sanctions in an effort to re-focus clients on the importance of following program requirements. The judge frequently softened the team's recommendation, giving the client a courtroom heart-to-heart, and clearly explaining that subsequent program violations would not be taken so lightly. The judge was quite consistent, however, in carrying out team recommended sanctions if clients wasted their second chance.

FTC Adherence to National Standards

The National Center on Addiction and Substance Abuse at Columbia University lists six main goals of family drug courts (National Center on Addiction and Substance Abuse, 1999, p. 62.) This family treatment court was measured against these six standards.

1. **Access to treatment**. This was one of the most beneficial attributes of the FTC program – immediate access to treatment. Any other available outpatient treatment program was commonly a 90-day wait to admission – longer for inpatient (unless pregnant).

FTC was the only program where fathers could enter into substance abuse treatment immediately.

2. **Coordination**. During the two-year team meeting observation, the team mentioned no less than forty-five resource referrals for FTC clients. Referrals ranged from transitional housing, to inpatient services, to parenting classes, to medical and mental health resources. While the services were numerous, none of them were co-located, each had a different set of program requirements, many had waiting lists, and the financial assistance that most clients needed to access some of the more critical services (e.g., medical and mental health care) was nearly non-existent.

   Team members, more than clients, were the ones who most benefited from inter-agency coordination. Through team oversight of clients and information sharing among agencies, team members felt they were uniformly better able to make informed decisions about clients' ability to achieve sobriety and care for their children. Those clients who had few complicating factors (e.g., mental health issues, chronic homelessness) benefited from the service referrals provided by the program, such as housing or childcare services; but, as one FTC graduate stated:

   > Having all those people [FTC team] is great if you're doing good, but bad if you're doing bad.

3. **Accountability**. The FTC judge was extraordinary in this regard. At every court hearing she was prepared with each client's background, referring many times in court to previous conversations she had with the client and treatment team members, and expecting forward movement from everyone at each meeting. During her interview the judge asserted:

   > I'm a big believer in sanctions for treatment providers as well as team members. If clients don't get an answer, they feel ignored. We should hold ourselves to the same high standards we ask our clients to uphold. It's very important for program accountability.

One graduate recalled:

> The public defenders misplaced my paperwork and the judge made them find it.

Another graduate remembered:

> At my request, the judge went to the CWS worker and said, "You have no basis for the order."

(The order prevented supervised overnight visits with the children while the mother was allowed supervised daytime visits in the exact same setting). Soon thereafter, the client received an order allowing her to stay overnight with her children.

4. **Motivation**. The FTC judge had a strong conviction about rewarding clients' treatment progress, not just sanctioning them. The judge was the impetus behind the team solidifying a reward system for clients (i.e., rewarding the first, and every fifth "excellent" court report thereafter.) She was instrumental in obtaining gift and discount cards from local vendors, or free tickets to local events as rewards for clients. Each year the treatment team would devote program and personal funds to provide clients with a Christmas present. One year the team furnished each client with a disposable camera and paid for the development of each roll of film. Another year they gave clients generous gift cards, carefully selecting which store would be most appropriate. Discussions included which stores did not sell tobacco or alcohol.

5. **Informed decision-making**. All FTC team members identified this as the best aspect of the program. The judge spoke of the great benefit of having a full picture of a client's family when serving as both the dependency court and family treatment court judge. She felt it helped her develop a respectful relationship with families, and provided a greater ability to match services to their needs. Child welfare workers expressed a desire for this kind of accountability for all CWS clients. The family treatment court approach provided workers with more real time information, such

as a relapse, that allowed them to respond more quickly to the needs of the child. Public defenders appreciated the frequent access to treatment progress information as well as on-tap resource information for clients provided by CWS workers and GALs at weekly team meetings.

6. **Timely resolution of cases**. The FTC team struggled with this issue and began to address it in 2005. All of the team members felt that the children should be returned earlier in the client's program so there was ample time for the client to adjust to sober parenting while they had the full support of the program. The team felt that they may ultimately be setting clients up for failure by waiting until the final three months of the program to return the children to the parent – a significant adjustment with little time to figure out and settle into a workable routine.

   As discussed in Chapter 10, FTC graduates in this study had similar lengths of open child dependency cases as the comparison group and those who opted out of the program (roughly 20 months). The difference in the resolution of dependency issues that did emerge was that program graduates were reunited with their children at a much higher rate (86%) than were any of the other groups, whose family reunification rates ranged from 11-25%.

CHAPTER 12

Conclusions and Implications

This family treatment court was fortunate to have a group of motivated, forward-thinking, dedicated and compassionate professionals who were responsible for this program. A family treatment court cannot be successful without a core group of devoted individuals who are willing to work together to address a devastating problem, and to have the courage to deliberate conscientiously over matters on which individual agencies generally disagree. Having individuals especially suited for this type of work is only the first step, however. Over the two-year observation period, the FTC team referenced some forty-five service providers when discussing necessary support services for clients. The drawback associated with this abundance of services providers was the long waiting lists to access them and/or the lack of funding for important "non-treatment" issues. In effect, while services other than substance abuse recovery were "offered," they were often difficult (if not impossible) to obtain. This reality makes it very difficult for both clients and programs to succeed in their efforts.

Family treatment court client needs are often immediate and always complex. When the only services they can access are sobriety maintenance, it is difficult to realize much progress in a meaningful recovery while stalled in every other aspect of life (e.g., parenting, mental health, housing, steady income). With the stressors these clients typically experience on a daily basis now under the microscope of a family treatment court team, relapse rates and program discharges/opt outs will remain substantial (50% for this study cohort) until the wide range of issues clients generally face can be addressed adequately by a full-service treatment program. This includes a family treatment court case manager who can assist in and advocate for client receipt of services. Freeman-Wilson (2003) observes that successful drug courts are able to tailor treatment to the needs of the individual clients participating in their programs. Drug courts must be able to assess and provide treatment for a wide range of issues, not just substance abuse (p. 24). The most commonly ignored of these issues is mental health. Federal funding for drug courts could be more effectively used if it were possible to remove the rule that prevents drug treatment court money from being used for mental health purposes. As previously stated, among people whose primary disorder is drug abuse, mood disorders were 4.7 times more prevalent compared with the general population (Regier, Farmer, Rae, Locke, Keith, Judd, et al., 1990). For FTC clients, 40% reported that treatment for psychiatric or emotional problems was "extremely important" to them at program entry.[26] However, only 6% of FTC clients reported they were receiving mental health services at program entry.

Medical research continues to find a close association between substance abuse and depression. A 2004 study found positron emission tomography (PET) images of brain activity in patients in acute withdrawal from methamphetamine use show changes strikingly similar to those of patients with known depressive and anxiety disorders (Rosack, 2004; Also see Alia-Klein, Parvaz, Woicik, Konova, Maloney , Shumay & Wang, et al., (2011) for PET scan information on cocaine users). Researchers believe the new brain scan radiological images offer empirical evidence that mood symptoms must be assessed—and adequately treated—to address methamphetamine abuse effectively, and quite likely other substances as well. Lead author Edythe London stated the major implication of their research, "Treating methamphetamine addicts typically focuses on addressing drug craving These PET images pinpoint, for the first time, abnormal brain activity that is closely linked to symptoms of depression and anxiety. Targeting these complicating conditions as part of a more comprehensive treatment program may improve success rates for methamphetamine addiction therapy" (Rosack, 2004). The evidence is clear that until mental health is treated and addressed on par with substance abuse

---

[26] It should be noted that of those clients who perceived treatment for psychological or emotional problems as "extremely" important at program entry, nearly 64% of them did not graduate from the program.

disorders, failure rates of clients and programs will continue to be considerable.

The best chance for clients with multiple challenges appears to exist in a system that does not require the shifting of treatment goals between service settings and providers (Hills, 2000, p. 11). Family treatment courts are helpful in this regard because treatment providers frequently communicate with each other concerning client treatment objectives. However, adding a mental health specialist on staff would likely benefit any family drug treatment court. It would provide clients with the opportunity to establish a long-term relationship with the provider that could engender trust, and thus encourage clients to stay with their course of prescription treatment and/or psychotherapy longer. It would also facilitate a level of comfort with clients to discuss pharmaceutical alternatives if their current course is not working for them. Privacy policies would need to be in place, however, to specify parameters for sharing information with the treatment team (e.g., whether a client has discontinued their mental health treatment course), and protecting client confidentiality (e.g., if the client is experiencing drug dreams and has concerns they may trigger a relapse). The power of relationship that is exhibited frequently throughout this and other studies should be an integral part of this crucial aspect of treatment.

Another area where FTC clients needed better services was in job training. Job training programs that keep clients on waiting lists for years is of little use to parents who need a living wage immediately to support their families. FTC clients are frequently referred to the Division of Vocational Rehabilitation (DVR) whose client placement priority is as follows:

1. Chemically dependent/mental health/developmentally disabled
2. Chemically dependent/mental health or Chemically dependent/developmentally disabled
3. Chemically dependent

Again, because few FTC clients qualified for *serious* mental health issues (e.g, schizophrenia or bi-polar disorder), but instead tended to suffer from depression or anxiety, it negatively affected their ability to receive employment assistance. Their acknowledged drug-dependence was not enough of a disability to warrant them priority employment training. As such, many clients had to take minimum wage jobs that held little interest or promise for working parents.

As previously discussed, the availability of safe, affordable, sober housing is essential to family treatment court clients. Often, clients must move from their existing homes because their family members, partners, or neighbors were using drugs. Housing assistance that only moves a parent from one substance-using environment to another, because sober housing is too expensive, does little to help a parent in recovery. One year after opening, the only transitional facility that allowed couples and children to live together increased the damage deposit from $350 to $600 due to tenant damage to the building – an impossible amount to produce for many families in crisis.

The low-income housing program, while comprehensive, had a long waiting list, and some clients perceived it as a lot more 'hoop-jumping.'

> The program has a 1-year program, but it's hard. You have twice a week check-ins, you have to meet once a week with a case manager, and take life skills classes twice a month.

> We tried the program first for housing, but it would have added more stress to our lives.

Others clients saw it differently:

> The program requires you take two 2-hour classes every month, meet with a case manager once a week, and meet with the supervisor once a month. To change your whole life, that's not asking for very much.

> I was stubborn and got my housing on my own. I should've went through the program, then I wouldn't have all these housing problems.

The housing program provided 90-day emergency shelter for homeless clients who could move to the program's transitional housing program for up to one year. Clients could then be eligible for the program's housing subsidy program for permanent housing for up to one year, thus providing housing assistance for over two years.

Childcare (particularly pre-school) and transportation services appeared to be fairly readily accessible to FTC clients due to the abundance of child-focused programs funded at all levels of government, and CWS' provision of free bus passes or monthly gas stipend for clients.

Aftercare and Relapse

There is a growing recognition by all drug courts that clients need continuing aftercare and a variety of transitional services – particularly relating to housing and employment issues – to increase the chances that drug court treatment successes are sustained (Harrell & Goodman, 1999, p. 35). Aftercare should be available following graduation and, ideally, be supplemented with a mentoring program or alumni association for long-term support, recovery, and ongoing healthy child development (Earp, 2004, p. 41). One of the FTC treatment counselors noted this as an advantage of successive FTC client groups:

> The first group of graduates didn't have a mentoring component. The second class just began to have a mentoring component, but this third (current) class really got and practiced the mentoring.

Unfortunately, once FTC clients graduated from the program they were no longer eligible for any type of funding from the program.

Of the small proportion of substance abusers that complete twelve months or more of treatment, about one-half of those remain abstinent for a year following discharge from treatment.[27] McLellan, Lewis, O'Brien, & Kleber (2000) observed that one-year post-discharge follow-up studies typically show that only 40% to 60% of patients are continuously abstinent, although an additional 15% to 30% have not resumed dependent use (p. 1693). While perhaps showing some promise for treatment, these modest figures may be inadequate for

---

[27] See Gainy, Wells, Hawkins, & Catalano (1993) finding 80% to 90% of drug treatment clients drop out within a year. Also see Satel (1999: 2) concluding that 80% to 90% of addicts leave treatment by the end of the first year.

serving public safety and public health objectives and are unlikely to sit well with policymakers or the public at large.

Interestingly, predictive measures may also be available to identify which clients will be most in need of aftercare. NIDA-supported investigators have found that functional magnetic resonance imaging (fMRI) of the brain performed during a psychological test can predict with high accuracy whether an individual will relapse following treatment for methamphetamine abuse. Previous studies by this same research team showed that poor choices made by drug abusers correlate to distinctive patterns of activity in some areas of the brain. The research team hypothesized that activity patterns in those regions might also be associated with relapse to drug abuse, which involves similarly destructive decisions. Their study revealed a characteristic pattern of brain activity in methamphetamine-abusing men who relapsed within one to three years after completing treatment, and a different pattern in men who did not. "The most striking aspect of this result is that the fMRI pattern has 90% accuracy in predicting outcome." Researchers using this approach assert, "The differences in brain activity are pronounced, with little overlap" (Paulus, Tapert, & Schuckit, 2005).

Of the forty-four clients who graduated during the study period, twelve (27%) are known to have relapsed within two years. Of those twelve graduates who relapsed:

- Four returned to the FTC treatment provider, asking for help to return to sobriety. Three were placed in the treatment provider's regular outpatient program to help them get back on track, and the fourth was accepted back into FTC, but was not able to complete the program.
- Three were monitored by TASC (regular UA screening) as requested by CPS, without returning to treatment; however, all the children had alternate living arrangements.
- Two became homeless and one gave birth to another child who was immediately placed into foster care. All three ultimately lost custody of their children to the state (two never having their children returned to their care since entering the program), and all three had either serious and debilitating mental health or developmental disability issues.

- One graduate was suspected of use, but the child resides with the other parent.
- One graduate was able to return to their partner and child after completing an inpatient program as the partner had successfully graduated the program and was reunified with the child.

In sum, this rigorous, extended treatment program is difficult to sell in an environment that offers so many abbreviated programs that demand much less accountability than FTC. Parents with developmental disabilities and/or co-occurring disorders are better off seeking out these other programs where their life skills are less likely to be under such pointed scrutiny, as none of the treatment options adequately address their "non-addiction" issues.

As expected, relapse was part of recovery. Both graduates and early outs relapsed (as measured by dirty UAs) at similar rates. Collectively during their enrollment in the program, the "early out" group missed more UAs and treatment meetings than did graduates. The early out group was also granted higher rates of excused absences by treatment counselors than were program graduates. It was clear the team struggled with how much pressure to apply in each situation to motivate, but not devastate, clients' progress toward sobriety.

Advantages of the FTC Program

The most advantageous aspect of the FTC program was the provision of immediate access to treatment. A close second was the ability for clients to build relationships with their treatment team and a judge who held the client and the team similarly accountable for the ultimate success of clients. One program graduate recalled:

> When I entered the program, I thought they were going to judge me, but they didn't, they were completely supportive of me. I felt blessed to have all the people supporting me. It's scary when you're alone.

Another FTC program graduate stated:

> In the first 1-2 months working with CWS we had a personality conflict with the CWS worker. We felt bad about what we had done (using drugs), and didn't want people telling us how bad we should feel. We didn't need people saying, "shame, shame."

Once in the program clients noted a change in perception of the AAG from one of dislike (due to the AAG's role in the initial shelter care hearing of arguing against the parents keeping their child), to one of respect:

> Then you start seeing her [AAG] every week in court. I never felt there was a tone that she was against me or judging me. I realized she was just doing her job. It reinforced that everybody wanted us to succeed, and they weren't feeling like, "once a screw up, always a screw up."

Another strength of the program was that FTC team members believe in the program. Because every one of them had years of experience in 'business as usual' dependencies, team members appreciated the program aspects of hands-on, high accountability, and timely exchange of information among agencies who participated in the family drug court treatment program. Every team member commented on this during their interviews, calling FTC the "Cadillac" of treatment programs where clients could enter treatment immediately and have access to a variety of support services. Representative team comments included the following:

> The faster you get people into treatment (especially while they're in crisis), the better they are likely to do.

> FTC shows how a non-adversarial system can work, how advantageous it can be to the system as well as to the clients.

> Meetings once a week with treatment staff, to have access to them, there's a lot less phone tag. The ability to staff cases every other week is good. I've advocated for this modified

> model for ALL our cases, but it will never happen. It's too time- and labor-intensive.
>
> Clients having so much visibility and accountability to the court. In regular dependency cases, clients go to court every 5-6 months.
>
> I like the idea that we get to know the people (clients). You feel like you've accomplished something. For non-FTC clients, you're so removed. The only times you see those parents is in a contested hearing, every 6 months.
>
> CWS workers have increased accountability (to the court and their clients). In FTC, we work with relapsed/using clients a lot more liberally than we normally would.
>
> Families are getting immediate access to treatment. People are in treatment before their fact-finding.
>
> Having one treatment provider in FTC [as opposed to several treatment providers in other jurisdictions] is a positive because treatment can answer all the program questions.
>
> In non-FTC cases, it's more contentious between the public defenders and the CWS workers. Plus, we get the plum clients in FTC.

Other team members commented on the second chances clients were given as the team recognized relapse as a part of recovery:

> It takes a lot to get discharged from this program. Clients are given a lot of chances, and they should.
>
> We're giving clients more chances, which is good for clients.
>
> We move quickly on the front end (getting clients into treatment), but we're slow on the back end because clients are

> given lots of time in the beginning [to acclimate to the program/sobriety/parenting].

FTC also helped clients who were doing well in recovery avoid criminal drug-related charges by providing the prosecutor with treatment progress reports on the client's behalf that demonstrated the client's willingness and ability to rehabilitate themselves. One graduate noted:

> I had a felony possession. Thank God I was in treatment. They saved my butt. When I graduated [from FTC] I sent them [the federal prosecutor] my paperwork and they dropped the charges.

Another graduate stated a similar experience:

> FTC helped me get a decent deal for the criminal charges. While in the program, I was released from jail to go to treatment, school, meetings, visitations, and church.

One graduate who noted that the program was quite difficult also concluded:

> It (FTC) made the difference between me being here [reunified, supporting his/her family], or me being in prison.

Graduates noted the advantage of their FTC child welfare worker's ability to move them to the top of the housing list, convincing housing providers that he had the most highly desirable, sober families who had more than twice the sober time of the usual 3-month outpatient program clients. Graduates also listed free bus passes or gas stipends, furniture and clothing for themselves and their children, and assistance with filling out financial aid forms for school as aspects of the program they appreciated most. Another support service several graduates mentioned was the program's financial help in getting their driver's licenses reinstated – a $150 fee.

Graduates who received family preservation services while in the program always described their counselor in glowing terms. FTC clients felt the counselor was their advocate, listening to their concerns regarding parenting, housing and CWS. FTC clients appreciated the support counselors offered in the way of supplies, clothing and transportation for themselves and their children, and liked the fact that someone would offer services to them in their own home. Grant, Ernst, & Streissguth (1996), assert that child welfare officials need many strategies to motivate mothers, and the use of paraprofessionals to engage parents in treatment is a particularly promising innovation. Help and encouragement from a woman who has "been there" may resonate with an addicted woman in a unique and powerful way.

One Judge or Two?

This family treatment court elected to have just one judge preside over both the dependency and the family treatment courts. The FTC judge observed:

> I think having the same judge preside over treatment and dependency court is a wonderful idea. When you start stretching out the parents among too many programs, it gets taxing on them. If you get two judges with slightly different philosophies, it can be bad for the clients. Plus, (as a dependency court judge) I need to know what's going on in treatment.

One AAG expressed similar views:

> I don't see any cons about one judge being both the FTC and dependency judge for the same clients. Before FTC, the county had a different commissioner hearing dependencies every six months. Kids were languishing. It was a mess. The more a judge knows about a case, the better. Sobriety does not equal good parenting. If you split those decisions between two judges, one would look at the parents and how well they're doing in treatment, and the other judge would look at just the child. That's like saying having too much information is bad.

Interestingly, child welfare workers tended to feel differently:

> I still like the idea of separate courts. I think it would work better if there were a little more clarity between FTC court and dependency court. Judge [] having clients air their dirty laundry in treatment court and not dependency court -- it seems like we're beating a dead horse a lot.

As evidenced through their comments during treatment team meetings regarding separating 'treatment' issues from 'dependency' issues, the public defenders would also prefer to have separate judges for treatment and dependency matters.

In another family treatment court in the state, dependency issues are not discussed during treatment team meetings; the focus was solely on the parents' sobriety. One of the FTC founding members observed the following:

> Another jurisdiction's family treatment court is better about returning kids. The judges there rely more on their perception of the parents, rather than the DCFS recommendations. Our FTC is more cautious, relying more heavily on DCFS recommendations.

The other FTC is also viewed as more punitive than the FTC in this study, operating more like a felony drug court, without graduated sanctions, instead building up large quantities of community service hours.

The clients who ultimately succeeded in the program seemed to benefit from a single judge overseeing both their treatment and dependency cases. The most integral aspect of life course theory – relationship – clearly manifested itself in this regard. When a parent is dealt the devastating blow of having their children removed from them, they predictably come into the family court system angry and afraid. If instead of being met with a detached magistrate, indifferent service providers, and an isolated existence between bi-annual court dates, the parents encounter a team of professionals who will listen to them, encourage them, and match them with supportive services, those parents are more likely to engage longer in the program and ask for help when they relapse.

In contrast, clients who were unsuccessful in the program likely would have preferred more than one judge overseeing their case. One client who continued to struggle in the program no matter what accommodations were provided, and who was very experienced with the dependency court system, once interrupted the judge's ruling on her sanctions to announce she was opting out of the program. The judge sternly replied, *"You can opt out, but your case will remain with me and I am very familiar with the history."* The AAG added, *"And Your Honor, she still needs to complete her jail and essay sanctions"* [before opting out of the program]. It is unlikely that a two-judge system could either hold clients as accountable or understand the true achievement of their recovery to the level a single-judge system could.

Based on this philosophy, this court was moving towards a Unified Family Court (UFC) System – one family, one judge. Any matter before the court involving a family – be it dependency, domestic violence, juvenile delinquency, or drug use issues – would be heard by one judge. While this is a promising development, the jurisdiction must overcome the deficiencies still found in this innovative practice of jurisprudence. A 2004 survey of unified family courts found just 61% provided psychiatric treatment services to their clients, 61% provided individual therapy, and only 56% provided job placement services to their clients (Bozzomo & Scolieri, 2004).[28] The high rates of co-occurring disorders in this population, combined with their limited job skills make these services crucial to family treatment court client success.

Disadvantages of FTC Program

Disadvantages of the program for team members included FTC weekly meeting with court days selected by the court, and frequent accountability with the court. One public defender observed the following:

> The difficulty with the FTC program for public defenders is the regularity of it. Every other Monday is shot. It messes up two potential trial days per month. The other public defender and I can trade, but it's a pain.

---

[28] Survey participants: AL, CA, DE, FL, GA, HI, KY, MD, MO, NH, NC, OR, PA, RI, SC, WA and DC.

The GAL office noted the increased workload brought on by FTC clients:

> GALs write reports every three months for FTC clients, every six months for non-FTC clients.

Child welfare workers too described the pressure to have significant progress reports for the court every two weeks, particularly with high-need, low-motivation clients (See RCW 13.34.174 delineating state progress report requirements).

Clients listed different attributes of the program they felt needed improvement. During interviews, some graduates noted that parents with younger children were often allowed by the team to have their children returned sooner than those with school age or teenage children.

> Some people were in the program 60-90 days with babies and were getting their kids back. What's the difference between a baby living with his Mom, and a school age child living with his Mom? If you have older kids, your kids aren't returned that fast. If you know people who want to come to this program and have school age kids, tell them not to do it.

Clients also expressed a desire to have professional help completing their parenting plans with their children's other parent. Clients had to depend on friends to help them complete the complex legal forms that were a required part of reunification. One graduate commented:

> The program needs to start clients a little earlier on with the parenting plan, about ½ way through the program. Also, they don't have anybody to help you with the parenting plan, and they don't tell you how to do it. They don't tell you that you have to do it until the last minute.

Another graduate stated:

> I just wish they [the public defenders] could help with the parenting plan. They're not allowed to help. You have to get

> your own (family law) attorney. I don't know how to word the parenting plan, or who bears the expense. My court date was moved up a week and the parenting plan has to be done before the dependency will be dismissed.

Conclusion

Judge Charles McGee (2000), who initiated the first family treatment court, insightfully observed the following, "There is a serious question in the minds of many judges and treatment professionals as to whether it is truly possible for a person who is heavily involved with drugs and/or alcohol to become both sober and learn how to be a nurturing parent and resolve interpersonal conflicts with husbands, boyfriends, or children, within the one-year period under the ASFA guidelines" (p. 24). The population of family treatment court clients come to the state's attention largely because they are poor and do not have the means or access to resources believed to help people overcome their drug-dependence, not because they use drugs at higher rates than more affluent parents. Clearly, a parent lost to substance abuse and the accompanying chaotic lifestyle that replaces a child-focused approach to parenting must be re-directed toward their parenting priorities or relinquish the child to the healthiest possible environment available. However, as McGee aptly observes, "Unless the courts are willing to help create and monitor comprehensive services for families, then an excellent legal argument can be made that the state has violated its covenant to perform reasonable efforts to preserve and reunify the family within the tougher time lines set out in the [ASFA] Act" (p. 24). The uncomfortable truth is that clients who already have an outside, sober support system in place to help them address all of the challenges listed above are apt to do better in treatment. Clients need to bring many of their own resources with them into treatment in order to succeed. One FTC treatment counselor observed:

> If a client doesn't have family or other social support, it's difficult; especially during the first phase when clients are encouraged to focus on treatment and not employment.

Family treatment courts are the best programs available to parents whose drug involvement has contributed to their children being taken into state custody. For all its shortcomings, there is nothing that matches the attention and accountability exercised towards client recovery. However, family drug courts appear to remain in the beginning stages of comprehensive care for extremely high-needs clients. Devoting more attention and resources toward the mental health, housing, and employment needs of clients is a necessary next step for the family treatment court phenomenon (See Worcel, Furrer, Green & Rhodes, 2006, p. III). Further, the one common denominator that all of the FTC graduates named when asked for whom this program would work best was those parents who were "ready" or "motivated" to get clean. They praised the program for helping them get clean and reunify their families, but concluded that the best program in the world will not help (graduates believed, *could* not help) someone who was not ready to stop using and get clean.

> I was ready to stop using when I entered the program.
>
> I would recommend the FTC program to people who are ready to change.
>
> This program is great for people who are ready for treatment. If you're not done using, no program is going to help. Nothing is going to help you if you're not ready to quit (using).
>
> I would recommend FTC to anyone who is ready for treatment. If they're not ready, they need to go to inpatient, because most counselors (in inpatient programs) are ex-addicts.
>
> If a person is not ready, treatment won't work.

For parents considering treatment court, some may not feel ready or capable of personal and family recovery until they are able to spend some time with others like them, who face the uniquely difficult phenomenon of drug-dependence and parenthood. The challenge for treatment teams is to get and keep a parent in treatment long enough for this realization to occur.

Obstacles in Family Treatment Court Research

A 1999 Urban Institute evaluation of the implementation of three family treatment courts cited many of the challenges particular to this emerging model (client confidentiality, juggling the rights of the parent and the welfare of the child, the use of sanctions, and extensive service needs), noting that any effort to seriously evaluate family treatment courts would run up against a number of obstacles, including the need to track multiple parties (parents and children) and serious confidentiality restrictions (Harrell & Goodman, 1999).[29] Such was indeed the case for this evaluation. Three years of meetings with various levels and departments of the State Department of Social and Health Services, numerous drafts of research applications, access approved, then denied, then partially approved is just a brief summary of the obstacles associated with this research. Future evaluations should plan accordingly for these setbacks.

Postscript

Recent correspondence with the family treatment court team members (2011) revealed that the family treatment court shut down in late 2008 or early 2009 due to funding issues, and no program replaced it. These parental substance abuse dependency cases returned to regular dependency court - assigned to one of the court commissioners and

---

[29] Also citing immediate outcomes [for children] include the duration and number of foster care episodes while the case is before the court and the final placement is pending (parents, in kinship foster care, and in foster care). Longer-term outcomes for those placed with their parents include the percentage named in subsequent abuse or neglect petitions, and, for those in which parental rights were terminated, the percentage adopted. Immediate outcomes [for parents] include treatment graduation/failure, substance abuse and participation in aftercare following case termination, perceptions of fairness of court process, effects of process on treatment motivation and retention, and assessment of the relationship between family drug court services and reductions in problems faced by parents.

providing services including evaluations, UAs and treatment, which, in part, is still provided by the drug treatment provider in this study.

The judge from this study reported that when she rotated out of the FTC, "Unfortunately, I think I saw just about every parent we had in FTC show up in the criminal court on new drug related charges. It was discouraging."

These circumstances may speak to the fact that FTC clients were so busy receiving sobriety treatment while in the program that they could not devote any time to advancing their education or job skills – two important aspects in entering into and maintaining a conventional, sober lifestyle. Treatment courts should examine extending services beyond sobriety treatment and housing to connect clients with life skills services while still receiving the support of the FTC treatment team.

APPENDIX

Washington State Statutes

RCW 9A.42.010 Definitions: (1) "Basic necessities of life" means food, water, shelter, clothing, and medically necessary health care, including but not limited to health-related treatment or activities, hygiene, oxygen, and medication.

RCW 9A.42.020 Criminal Mistreatment in the First Degree. (1) A parent of a child, the person entrusted with the physical custody of a child or dependent person, a person who has assumed the responsibility to provide to a dependent person the basic necessities of life, or a person employed to provide to the child or dependent person the basic necessities of life is guilty of criminal mistreatment in the first degree if he or she recklessly, as defined in RCW 9A.08.010, causes great bodily harm to a child or dependent person by withholding any of the basic necessities of life.

RCW 9A.42.030 Criminal Mistreatment in the Second Degree. . . guilty of criminal mistreatment in the second degree if he or she recklessly, as defined in RCW 9A.08.010, either (a) creates an imminent and substantial risk of death or great bodily harm, or (b) causes substantial bodily harm by withholding any of the basic necessities of life.

RCW 9A.42.035 Criminal Mistreatment in the Third Degree. A person is guilty of the crime of criminal mistreatment in the third degree if the person either: (a) With criminal negligence, creates an imminent and substantial risk of substantial bodily harm to a child or dependent person by withholding any of the basic necessities of life; or (b) With criminal negligence, causes substantial bodily harm to a child or dependent person by withholding any of the basic necessities of life.

RCW 9A.42.037 Criminal Mistreatment in the Fourth Degree. A person is guilty of the crime of criminal mistreatment in the fourth degree if the person either: (a) With criminal negligence, creates an imminent and substantial risk of bodily injury to a child or dependent person by withholding any of the basic necessities of life; or (b) With criminal negligence, causes bodily injury or extreme emotional distress manifested by more than transient physical symptoms to a child or dependent person by withholding the basic necessities of life.

RCW 13.34.020 Legislative Declaration of Family Unit as Resource to be Nurtured — Rights of child. (1990). The legislature declares that the family unit is a fundamental resource of American life which should be nurtured. Toward the continuance of this principle, the legislature declares that the family unit should remain intact unless a child's right to conditions of basic nurture, health, or safety is jeopardized. When the rights of basic nurture, physical and mental health, and safety of the child and the legal rights of the parents are in conflict, the rights and safety of the child should prevail. In making reasonable efforts under this chapter, the child's health and safety shall be the paramount concern. The right of a child to basic nurturing includes the right to a safe, stable, and permanent home and a speedy resolution of any proceeding under this chapter.

RCW 13.34.138 - Review hearings – Findings (1) . . , the status of all children found to be dependent shall be reviewed by the court at least every six months from the beginning date of the placement episode or the date dependency is established, whichever is first, at a hearing in which it shall be determined whether court supervision should continue. The initial review hearing shall be an in-court review and shall be set six months from the beginning date of the placement episode or no more than ninety days from the entry of the disposition order, whichever comes first. The initial review hearing may be a permanency planning hearing when necessary to meet the time frames set forth in RCW 13.34.145(3) or 13.34.134. The review shall include findings regarding the agency and parental completion of disposition plan requirements, and if necessary, revised permanency time limits. This review shall consider both the agency's and parent's efforts that demonstrate consistent measurable progress over time in meeting the disposition plan requirements. The requirements for the initial review hearing, including the in-court requirement, shall be accomplished within existing resources. The supervising agency shall provide a foster parent, pre-adoptive parent, or relative with notice of, and their right to an opportunity to be heard in, a review hearing pertaining to the child, but only if that person is currently providing care to that child at the time of the hearing. This section shall not be construed to grant party status to any person who has been provided an opportunity to be heard. (a) A child shall not be returned home at the review hearing unless the court finds that a reason for removal as set forth in RCW 13.34.130 no longer exists. The parents, guardian, or legal custodian shall report to the court the efforts they have made to correct the conditions which led to removal. If a child is returned, casework supervision shall continue for a period of six months, at which time there shall be a hearing on the need for continued intervention.

RCW 13.34.145 Permanency plan required — Permanency planning hearing — Time limits. (3) A permanency planning hearing shall be held in all cases where the child has remained in out-of-home care for at least nine months and an adoption decree, guardianship order, or permanent custody order has not previously been entered. The hearing shall take place no later than twelve months following commencement of the current placement episode. (11) . . . the status of all dependent children shall continue to be reviewed by the court at least once every six months, in accordance with RCW 13.34.138, until the dependency is dismissed. Prior to the second permanency planning hearing, the agency that has custody of the child shall consider whether to file a petition for termination of parental rights.

RCW 13.34.165 Civil contempt. (1) Failure by a party to comply with an order entered under this chapter is civil contempt of court as provided in RCW 7.21.030(2)(e). (2) The maximum term of confinement that may be imposed as a remedial sanction for contempt of court under this section is confinement for up to seven days.

RCW 13.34.174 Order of Alcohol or Substance Abuse Diagnostic Investigation and Evaluation — Treatment plan — Reports. (1) The provisions of this section shall apply when a court orders a party to undergo an alcohol or substance abuse diagnostic investigation and evaluation. (2) The facility conducting the investigation and evaluation shall make a written report to the court stating its findings and recommendations including family-based services or treatment when appropriate. If its findings and recommendations support treatment, it shall also recommend a treatment plan setting out: (a)

Type of treatment; (b) Nature of treatment; (c) Length of treatment; (d) A treatment time schedule; and (e) Approximate cost of the treatment.

The affected person shall be included in developing the appropriate treatment plan. The treatment plan must be signed by the treatment provider and the affected person. The initial written progress report based on the treatment plan shall be sent to the appropriate persons six weeks after initiation of treatment. Subsequent progress reports shall be provided after three months, six months, twelve months, and thereafter every six months if treatment exceeds twelve months. Reports are to be filed with the court in a timely manner. Close-out of the treatment record must include summary of pretreatment and post-treatment, with final outcome and disposition. The report shall also include recommendations for ongoing stability and decrease in destructive behavior.

RCW 13.34.176. Violation of Alcohol or Substance Abuse Treatment Conditions —Hearing — Notice — Modification of order. **(1) The court, upon receiving a report under RCW 13.34.174(4) or at the department's request, may schedule a show cause hearing to determine whether the person is in violation of the treatment conditions. All parties shall be given notice of the hearing. The court shall hold the hearing within ten days of the request for a hearing. At the hearing, testimony, declarations, reports, or other relevant information may be presented on the person's alleged failure to comply with the treatment plan and the person shall have the right to present similar information on his or her own behalf.**

(2) If the court finds that there has been a violation of the treatment conditions it shall modify the dependency order, as necessary, to ensure the safety of the child. The modified order shall remain in effect until the party is in full compliance with the treatment requirements.

RCW 26.12.170 Authority of Family Court Judges and Court Commissioners to Order or Recommend Services -- Report by Court of Child Abuse or Neglect. To facilitate and promote the purposes of this chapter, family court judges and court commissioners may order or recommend family court services, parenting seminars, drug and alcohol abuse evaluations and monitoring of the parties through public or private treatment services, other treatment services, the aid of physicians, psychiatrists, other specialists, or other services or may recommend the aid of the pastor or director of any religious denomination to which the parties may belong.

RCW 26.44.020 (12) "Abuse or neglect" means the injury, sexual abuse, sexual exploitation, negligent treatment, or maltreatment of a child by any person under circumstances which indicate that the child's health, welfare, and safety is harmed, excluding conduct permitted under RCW 9A.16.100. An abused child is a child who has been subjected to child abuse or neglect as defined in this section.

RCW 26.44.170(1) Alleged child abuse or neglect — Use of alcohol or controlled substances as contributing factor — Evaluation. (1) When, as a result of a report of alleged child abuse or neglect, an investigation is made that includes an in-person contact with the person who is alleged to have committed the abuse or neglect, there shall be a determination of whether it is probable that the use of alcohol or controlled substances is a contributing factor to the alleged abuse or neglect.

(3) If a determination is made under subsection (1) of this section that there is probable cause to believe abuse of alcohol or controlled substances has contributed to the child abuse or neglect, the department shall, within available funds, cause a comprehensive chemical dependency evaluation to be made of the person or persons so identified. The evaluation shall be conducted by a physician or persons certified under rules adopted by the department to make such evaluation. The department shall perform the duties assigned under this section within existing personnel resources.

RCW 26.44.195 Negligent treatment or maltreatment — Offer of services — Evidence of substance abuse — In-home services — Initiation of dependency proceedings. (Effective January 1, 2007.)

(2) When evaluating whether the child has been subject to negligent treatment or maltreatment, evidence of a parent's substance abuse as a contributing factor to a parent's failure to provide for a child's basic health, welfare, or safety shall be given great weight.

(3) If the child's parents, guardians, or legal custodians are available and willing to participate on a voluntary basis in in-home services, and the department determines that in-home services on a voluntary basis are appropriate for the family, the department may offer such services.

(6) Nothing in this section shall be construed to create in any person an entitlement to services or financial assistance in paying for services or to create judicial authority to order the provision of services to any person or family if

the services are unavailable or unsuitable or if the child or family is not eligible for such services.

References

Abbott, A. (1997). On the concept of turning point. *Comparative Social Research*, 16, 85-105.

Adoption and Safe Families Act (ASFA). (1997). (42 U.S.C. 603, 622, 629, 629a, 629b, 645, 653, 670-675, 677-679, 679b, 901, 1305, 1320a-9, 5111, 5113).

Alia-Klein N, Parvaz MA, Woicik PA, Konova AB, Maloney T, Shumay E, Wang R, Telang F, Biegon A, Wang GJ, Fowler JS, Tomasi D, Volkow ND, Goldstein RZ. (2011). Gene x disease interaction on orbitofrontal gray matter in cocaine addiction. *Archives of General Psychiatry*, 68(3):283-94.

American Association of Suicidology. (2003). *U.S.A. Suicide: 2003 Official Final Data.*

Anglin, M.D., Burke, C., Perrochet, B., Stamper, E., & Dawud-Noursi, S. (2000). History of the methamphetamine problem. *Journal of Psychoactive Drugs*, 32, 137-141.

Anti-Drug Abuse Act of 1988. (1988). Pub. L. No. 100-690, 102 Stat. 4181; Anti-Drug Abuse Act of 1986, Pub. L. No. 99-570, 100 Stat. 3207.

Barnowski, R., & Aos, S. (2003). *Washington State's drug courts for adult defendants: outcome evaluation and cost-benefit analysis.* Olympia: Washington State Institute for Public Policy.

Bays, J. (1990). Substance abuse and child abuse: impact of addiction on the child. *Pediatric Clinics of North America*, 37, 881-904.

Benda, B.B. (2005). Gender differences in life-course theory of recidivism: A survival analysis. *International Journal of Offender Therapy and Comparative Criminology*, 49, 325-342.

Besharov, D. (1990). Crack children in foster care. *Children Today*, 35, 21-25.

Biederman, J. (2000). Patterns of alcohol and drug use in adolescents can be predicted by parental substance use disorders. *Pediatrics*, 106, 792-797.

Blumberg, A. (1967). The practice of law as confidence game: Organizational cooptation of a profession. *Law & Society Review*, 1, 15-39.

Boeri, M.W., Sterk, C.E., & Elifson, K.W. (2006). Baby boomer drug users: Career phases, social control, and social learning theory. *Sociological Inquiry*, 76, 264–291.

Boldt, R. (2002). The adversary system and attorney role in the drug treatment court movement. In James L. Nolan, Jr. (ed.), *Drug Courts in Theory and in Practice* (pp. 115-124). New York: Aldine de Gruyter.

Bowers v. Hardwick. 478 U.S. 186 (1986).

Bozzomo, J. W., & Scolieri, G. (2004). A survey of unified family courts: An assessment of different jurisdictional models. *Family Court Review*, 42, 12-38.

Brewster, M. P. (2001). An evaluation of the Chester (PA) drug court program. *Journal of Drug Issues*, 31, 177-206.

Brunner, T. (2006). Personal communication with County ATR Program Manager, March 6, 2006.

Bureau of Justice Statistics Drug Court Clearinghouse, (2006). *Summary of juvenile/family drug court activity by state and county.* American University, Washington D.C..

Bureau of Justice Statistics Drug Court Clearinghouse. (July 2010). *Summary of juvenile/family drug court activity by state and county.* American University, Washington D.C.

Burrus, S. W. M., Mackin, J. R., & Aborn, J. A. (Aug. 2008). Baltimore City Family Recovery Program (FRC) Independent Evaluation: Outcome and Cost Report. A report to the Maryland Judiciary, Office of Problem-Solving Courts. NPC Research: Portland, OR.

Carey, S. M., & Waller, M. S. (Re-Release, March 2011). Oregon Drug Court Cost Study – Statewide Costs and Promising Practices: Final Report. Submitted to the Oregon Criminal Justice Commission. Portland, OR: NPC Research

Chaffin, M., Kelleher, K. & Hollenberg, J (1996).

Chasnoff, I.J. (1990). *Methodological issues in perinatal substance abuse.* Paper presented at the annual meeting of the National Association of Perinatal Addiction Research and Education, Chicago, IL

Chester, D.L., Jose, R.M., Aldlyami, E., King, H., & Moiemen, N.S. (2006). Non-accidental burns in children -- are we neglecting neglect? *Burns: Journal of the International Society for Burn Injuries*, 32, 222-228.

Child Abuse Prevention and Treatment Act (CAPTA). (2001). 42 U.S.C. 5106g.

Child Welfare League of America. (1998). *Alcohol and other drug survey of state child welfare agencies*. Washington, DC.

Children at the front: a different view of the war on alcohol and drugs. (1992). Washington D.C.: Child Welfare League of America.

Coleman, J.S. (1988). Social capital in the creation of human capital. *American Journal of Sociology*, 94, S95-S120.

Confronting the cycle of addiction and recidivism: A report to Chief Judge Judith S. Kaye. (2000). New York: New York State Commission on Drugs and the Courts.

Conners, N.A., Bradley, R.H., Mansell, L.W., Liu, J.Y., Roberts, T.J., Burgdorf, K., et al. (2003). Children of mothers with serious substance abuse problems: An accumulation of risks. *The American Journal of Drug and Alcohol Abuse*, 29, 743-758.

Cooper, C.S. (2003). *Drug courts -- just the beginning: Getting other areas of public policy in sync*. Prepared for the Middle Eastern-Mediterranean Summer Institute on Drug Use: Justice Programs Office, School of Public Affairs, American University, Washington D.C. 2003-2004.

Crandall, M., Chiu, B., & Sheehan, K. (2006). Injury in the first year of life: Risk factors and solutions for high-risk families. *The Journal of Surgical Research*, 133, 7-10.

Daily, A.C. (1993). Constitutional privacy and the just family. *Tulane Law Review*, 67, 955-1000.

Dakof, G.A., Cohen, J.B., Henderson, C.E., Duarte, E., Boustani, M., Blackburn, A., Venzer, E. & Hawes, S. (2010). A randomized pilot study of the Engaging Moms Program for family drug court. *Journal of Substance Abuse Treatment*, 38(3), 263-274.

Diagnostics and Statistical Manual of Mental Disorders, 4th ed. (2000). New York: American Psychiatric Association.

Doherty, E.E. (2006). Self-control, social bonds, and desistance: A test of life-course interdependence. *Criminology*, 44, 807–833.

Earls, F., Reich W, Jung K.G., & Cloninger R. (1988). Psychopathology in children of alcoholic and antisocial parents. *Alcoholism: Clinical and Experimental Research*, 12, 481-487.

Earp, B. (2004). *Family dependency treatment courts: Addressing child abuse and neglect cases using the drug court model*. Washington D.C.: U.S.

Department of Justice Office of Justice Programs, Bureau of Justice Assistance.

Edwards, L.P. & Ray, J.A. (Summer 2005). Judicial perspectives on family drug treatment courts. *Juvenile and Family Court Journal*, 54, 1-27.

Eisenstien, J. & Jacob, H. (1991). *Felony justice: An organizational analysis of criminal courts*, New York: University Press of America.

Elder, Jr., G. (1985). *Life course dynamics: Trajectories and transitions, 1968-1980*. New York: Cornell University Press.

Elder, Jr., G.H. (1998). Life course and human development. In William Damon (ed.), *Handbook of Child Psychology: Theoretical Models of Human Development, 5th edition* (pp. 939-91). New York: John Wiley & Sons.

Etienne, M. (2003). Remorse, responsibility, and regulating advocacy: making defendants pay for the sins of their lawyers. *New York University Law Review*, 78, 2103-2159.

Evaluation of the Suffolk Family Treatment Court. (2000). Child Welfare Training Program, Stony Brook School of Social Welfare, State University of New York.

Evan B. Donaldson Adoption Institute. (2002). *Foster Care Facts*.

Fabricius, V. V., Langa, M. M., & Wilson, K. K. (2008). An exploratory investigation of co-occurring substance-related and psychiatric disorders. *Journal of Substance Use*, 13(2), 99-114.

Fals-Stewart, W., O'Farrell, T.J., Feehan, M., Birchler, G.R., Tiller, S., & McFarlin, S.K. (2000). Behavioral couples' therapy versus individual-based treatment for male substance-abusing patients: An evaluation of significant individual change and comparison of improvement rates. *Journal of Substance Abuse Treatment*, 18, 249-254.

Fals-Stewart, W., Fincham, F.D., & Kelley, M. (2004). Substance-abusing parents' attitudes toward allowing their custodial children to participate in treatment: A comparison of mothers versus fathers. *Journal of Family Psychology*, 18, 666–671.

Festinger, D.S., Lamb, R.J., Kirby, K.C., & Marlowe, D.B. (1996). The accelerated intake: A method for increasing initial attendance to outpatient cocaine treatment. *Journal of Applied Behavioral Analysis*, 29. 387-389.

Festinger, D.S., Lamb, R.J., Kountz, M.R., Kirby, K.C., & Marlowe, D. (1995). Pretreatment dropout as a function of treatment delay and client variables. *Addictive Behaviors*, 20, 111-115.

Festinger, D.S., Lamb, R.J., Marlowe, D.B., & Kirby, K.C. (2002). From telephone to office: Intake attendance as a function of appointment delay. *Addictive Behaviors*, 27, 131-137.

Finnerty v. Boyett, 469 So. 2d 287 (1985).

Focus Group Meeting of HUD representatives, drug court judges and others. (2003). National Association of Drug Court Professionals. January 2003.

Foster, S.E., & Macchetto M.L. (1999). Symposium: Substance abuse, families and the courts: Legal and public health challenges. Article: Providing safe haven: The challenge to family courts in cases of child abuse and neglect by substance-abusing parents. *Journal of Health Care Law & Policy*, 3, 44-62.

Freeman-Wilson, K. National Drug Court Institute. (2003). *Critical issues for defense attorneys in drug court: Monograph series 4.* Washington D.C.:

Friedmann, P.D., Lemon, S.C. & Stein, M.D. (2001). Transportation and retention in outpatient drug abuse treatment programs. *Journal of Substance Abuse Treatment*, 21, 97-103.

Gainy, R.R. Wells, E.A., Hawkins, J.D., & Catalano, R.F. (1993). Predicting treatment retention among cocaine abusers. *International Journal of Addictions*, 28, 487-496.

Gallas, E. (2004). Comment: Endorsing religion: Drug courts and the 12-step recovery support program. *American University Law Review*, 53, 1063-1101.

Giannini, F. D., McMahon, T. J. & Suchman, N. E. (2001). Talking with Poppa: Qualitative analysis of a focus group done with fathers enrolled in methadone maintenance treatment. *Drug and Alcohol Dependence, 63* (Supp. 1), S54-S55.

Gittler, J. (2003). The American drug war, maternal substance abuse and child protection: A commentary. *Journal of Gender Race & Justice*, 7, 237-264.

Goldkamp, J. (2000). Article: The drug court response: Issues and implications for justice change. *Albany Law Review*, 63, 923-950.

Goldkamp, J.S., White, M., & Robinson, J. (2000). *Retrospective evaluation of two pioneering drug courts: phase I findings from Clark County, Nevada, and Multnomah County, Oregon - An interim report of the national evaluation of drug courts*. Philadelphia, PA: Crime & Justice Research Institute.

Grant, T.M., Ernst, C.C., & Streissguth, A.P. (1996). An intervention with high risk mothers who abuse alcohol and drugs: The Seattle Advocacy Model. *American Journal of Public Health*, 86, 1816-1818.

Grella, C.E. (1999). Women in residential drug treatment: Differences by program type and pregnancy. *Journal of Health Care for the Poor and Underserved*, 10, 216-229.

Grella, C.E., Polinsky, M.L., Hser, Y., & Perry, S.M. (1999). Characteristics of women-only and mixed-gender drug abuse treatment programs. *Journal of Substance Abuse Treatment*, 17, 37-44.

Grudzinskas, Jr. A.J., Clayfield, J.C., Roy-Bujnowski, K., Fisher, W.H., & Richardson, M.H. (2005). Integrating the criminal justice system into mental health service delivery: The Worcester Diversion Experience. *Behavioral Sciences and the Law* 23, 277-293.

Haack, M.R., (Ed.). (1997). *Drug dependent mothers and their children: Issues in public policy and public health.* New York: Springer Publishing Company.

Harrell, A. (2000). Evaluation of the D.C. Superior Court drug intervention programs. Washington D.C.: National Institute of Justice. [Research in brief].

Harrell, A., & Goodman, A. (1999). *Review of specialized family drug courts: key issues handling child abuse and neglect cases.* New York: The Urban Institute.

Hartwell, S. (2003). Deviance over the life course: The case of homeless substance abusers. *Substance Use & Misuse*, 38, 475-503.

Hills, H.A. (March, 2000). Creating effective treatment programs for persons with co-occurring disorders in the justice system. *Delmar, NY: GAINS Center.*

Hora, P., Schma. W.G., & Rosenthal, J.T. (1999). Therapeutic jurisprudence and the drug treatment court movement: Revolutionizing the criminal justice system's response to drug abuse and crime in America. *Notre Dame Law Review*, 74, 439-498.

Housing Opportunity Program Extension (HOPE) Act of 1996. (1996). (Public Law No. 104-120). Section 110 Statute 834 (Mar. 28, 1996) 42 U.S.C. Section 1437d(1)(5) 1997.

Hubbard, R. L., Craddock, S. G., & Anderson, J. (2003). Overview of 5-year follow-up outcomes in the Drug Abuse Treatment Outcome Studies (DATOS). *Journal of Substance Abuse Treatment*, *25*(3), 125-134.

Hubbard, R.L., Marsden, M.E., Rachal, J.V., Harwood, H.J., Cavanaugh, E.R., & Ginzburg, H.M. (1989). *Drug abuse treatment: A national study of effectiveness.* Chapel Hill, NC: University of North Carolina Press.

Humphries, D. (1999). *Crack Mothers: Pregnancy, drugs and the media.* Columbus, OH: Ohio State University Press.

Inciardi, J. A., McBride, D.C., Rivers, J.E. (1996). Drug control and the courts. *Drugs, Health, and Social Policy Series,* Volume 3. Newbury Park, CA: Sage Publications.

Jones, H. (2004). Testimony before the House Committee on Government Reform, Subcommittee on Criminal Justice, Drug Policy and Human Resources about measuring the effectiveness of drug addiction treatment, March 30, 2004.

Jones, K.T. (1999). Prenatal substance abuse: Oregon's progressive approach to treatment and child protection can support children, women and families. *Willamette Law Review*, 35, 797-818.

Judge, M.P. (1995). *Critical issues in the design and operation of a drug court program: Current and emerging: The defense function.* Washington D.C.: National Legal Aid & Defender Association.

Judicial Council of California & California Department of Alcohol & Drug Programs. (2002). *Drug court partnership (DCP) final evaluation report.*

Kandel, D., Huang, F., & Davies, M. (2001). Comorbidity between patterns of substance use dependence and psychiatric syndromes. *Drug and Alcohol Dependence* 64, 233– 241.

Kelleher, K., Chaffin, M., Hollenberg, J., & Fischer, E. (1994). Alcohol and drug disorders among physically abusive and neglectful parents in a community-based sample. *American Journal of Public Health*, 84, 1586-1591.

Kessler, R.C., Nelson, C. B., McGonagle, K. A., Edlund, M. J., Frank, R. G., & Leaf, P. J. (1996). The epidemiology of co-occurring addictive and mental disorders: Implications for prevention and service utilization. *American Journal of Orthopsychiatry* 66, 17–31.

Kittrie, N. (1971). *The right to be different: Deviance and enforced therapy.* New York: Penguin Books.

Kowalski, S. (1998). Looking for a solution: Determining fetal status for pregnant drug abuse prosecutions. *Santa Clara Law Review*, 38, 1255-1281.

Laub, John H. Nagin, D.S., & Sampson, R.J. (1998). Trajectories of change in criminal offending: Good marriages and the desistance process. *American Sociological Review*, 63, 225-238.

Mackin, J. R., Carey, S. M., Finigan, M. W., Lucas, L. M., Lambarth, C. H., Waller, M. S., Herrera Allen, T., Weller, J. M., & Linhares, B. (Dec. 2009). Maryland Problem-Solving Courts Evaluation, Phase III: Integration of Results from Process, Outcome, and Cost Studies Conducted 2007-2009. A report to the Maryland Judiciary, Office of Problem-Solving Courts. NPC Research: Portland, OR.

Mancuso, D., & Estee, S. (2003). *Washington State mental health services: Cost offsets and client outcomes technical report*. Washington State Department of Social and Health Services, Management Services Administration, Research and Data Analysis Division.

Markou, A, Kosten, T.R., Koob, G.F. (1998). Neurobiological similarities in depression and drug dependence: A self-medication hypothesis. *Neuropsychopharmacology*, 18, 135–174.

Marlowe, D.B. (2011). The Verdict on Drug Courts and Other Problem-Solving Courts *Chapman Journal of Scientific Justice, 2(1), 57-96.*

McCoy, C. (2003). Community courts and community justice: Commentary: The politics of problem-solving: An overview of the origins and development of therapeutic courts. *American Criminal Law Review*, 40, 1513-1529.

McGee, C., Merrigan, T., Parnham, J.J., & Smith, M.O. (2000). *Applying Drug Court Concepts in Juvenile and Family Court Environments: A Primer for Judges*. American University, Justice Programs Office, School of Public Affairs.

McLellan, A.T., Lewis, D.C., O'Brien, C.P., & Kleber, H.D. (2000). Drug dependence, a chronic medical illness: Implications for treatment, insurance, and outcomes evaluation. *Journal of the American Medical Association*, 284, 1689-1695.

McMahon, T.J. (2001). Finding Poppa: A comparative study of fathers enrolled in methadone maintenance treatment. *Drug and Alcohol Dependence, 63* (Supp. 1), S102-S103.

McMahon, T.J. (2002). *Drug dependence, psychological representations of fathering, and reproductive cognitions in the parenting processes of drug-addicted mothers and fathers.* Symposium conducted at the annual meeting of the College on Problems of Drug Dependence, Quebec City, Canada.

McMahon, T.J., & Giannini, F.D. (2003). Substance abusing fathers in family court: Moving from popular stereotypes to therapeutic jurisprudence. *Family Court Review*, 41, 337-353.

McMahon, T.J. & Rounsaville, B.J. (2002). Substance abuse and fathering: Adding Poppa to the research agenda. *Addiction*, 97, 337-351.

McMahon TJ, Winkel JD, Rounsaville BJ. (2007). Drug abuse and responsible fathering: a comparative study of men enrolled in methadone maintenance treatment. *Addiction*. 103(2):269-83.

McMahon TJ, Winkel JD, Suchman NE, Rounsaville BJ. (2007). Drug-abusing fathers: patterns of pair bonding, reproduction, and paternal involvement. *Journal of Substance Abuse Treatment*. 33(3):295-302.

Mears, D. P., Ploeger, M., & Warr, M. (1998). Explaining the gender gap in delinquency: Peer influence and moral evaluations of behavior. *Journal of Research in Crime and Delinquency*, 35, 251-266.

Meyer v. *Nebraska,* 262 U.S. 401, 399 (1923).

In re Moore, 470 So. 2d 1269, 1270 (Ala. Civ. App. 1985).

Module 5: Alcohol, Marijuana, and Inhalants. (2006). National Institute on Drug Abuse.

Morrison-Dore, M., & Doris, J. (1998). Preventing child placement in substance-abusing families: Research-informed practice. *Child Welfare* 77, 407-426.

Mueser K., Noordsy, D.L., Drake, R.E., Fox, L. (2003). *Integrated treatment for dual disorders: A guide to effective practice.* New York, Guilford Publishing.

Nagin, D.S., Pagani, L., Tremblay,R.E., & Vitaro, F. (2003). Life Course Turning Points: The effect of grade retention on physical aggression. *Development and Psychopathology,* 15, 343-361.

National Association of State Alcohol and Drug Abuse Directors, Inc (NASADAD).Testimony on FY 2010 Federal Funding for addiction Treatment, Prevention, Recovery Services and Research, Submitted to the House Appropriations Subcommittee on Labor, *Health and Human Services, Education and Related Agencies. 18 March 2009.*

National Center on Addiction and Substance Abuse at Columbia University. (2009). *Shoveling up II: The impact of substance abuse on federal, state, and local budgets.* The National Press Club, Washington D.C.

National Center on Addiction and Substance Abuse at Columbia University. (1999). *No safe haven: Children of substance-abusing parents.*

National Center on Child Abuse and Neglect. (1993). *Study of child maltreatment in alcohol abusing families: A report to Congress.* Washington D.C.

National Institute on Drug Abuse. (2005). *Stimulants.*

National Institute of Mental Health. (2001). *Suicide facts and statistics.*

National Low Income Housing Coalition (2011). Out of Reach: Renters Await the Recovery.

National Mental Health Association (2002). *State coalitions on coordination of treatment for co-occurring disorders briefing document.* Washington, D.C.

The national treatment improvement evaluation study 1991-1996. (1997). Substance Abuse and Mental Health Services Administration (SAMHSA), Center for Substance Abuse Treatment Program (CSAT).

National treatment improvement evaluation study, preliminary report: Persistent effects of substance abuse treatment – one year later. (1996). Center for Substance Abuse Treatment. Rockville, MD: Author, Substance Abuse and Mental Health Services Administration, U.S. Department of Health & Human Services.

Nielson, A.L. (1999). Testing Sampson and Laub's life course theory: Age, race/ethnicity, and drunkenness. *Deviant Behavior: An Interdisciplinary Journal*, 20, 129–151.

Nordlund, D.J. (2004). *Chemical dependency treatment reduces emergency room costs and visits: Washington State supplemental security income recipients.* Washington State Department of Health and Social Services, Research and Data Analysis Division.

Oberman, M. (1992). Substance use during pregnancy: Legal and social responses: Sex, drugs, pregnancy, and the law: Rethinking the problems of pregnant women who use drugs. *Hastings Law Journal*, 42, 505-534.

O'Connell, D.J. (2003). Investigating latent trait and life course theories as predictors of recidivism among an offender sample. *Journal of Criminal Justice*, 31, 455-467.

Office of Justice Programs Drug Court Clearinghouse and Technical Assistance Project. (2000). *Family drug court activity update: Summary information.* Washington D.C.

Olmstead, T., & Sindelar, J.L. (2004). To what extent are key services offered in treatment programs for special populations? *Journal of Substance Abuse Treatment*, 27, 9-15.

Oro, A.S., & Dixon, S.D. (1987). Perinatal cocaine and methamphetamine exposure: Maternal and neonatal correlates. *Journal of Pediatrics*, 110, 571-578

Osher, F.C. & Drake, R.E. (1996). Reversing a history of unmet needs: Approaches to care for persons with co-occurring addictive and mental disorders. *American Journal of Orthopsychiatry*, 66, 4–12.

Osterling, K. L., & Austin, M. J. (2008). Substance abuse interventions for parents involved in the child welfare system: Evidence and implications. *Journal of Evidence-Based Social Work*, *5*, 157–189.

Paltrow, L. & Jack, K. (2010). Pregnant women, junk science, and zealous defense. National Association of Criminal Defense Lawyers, Inc., *The Champion* 34(30).

Paltrow, L. (1999). Punishment and prejudice: Judging drug-using pregnant women. In J.E. Hanigsberg & S. Ruddick (eds.), *Mother Troubles, Rethinking Contemporary Maternal Dilemmas* (pp. 59-77). Boston, MA: Beacon Press.

Petit, M.R., & Curtis, P.A. (1997). *Child abuse and neglect: A look at the states.* Arlington, VA: Child Welfare League of America (CWLA) Press.

Paulus, M.P., Tapert, S.F., & Schuckit, M.A. (2005). Neural activation patterns of methamphetamine-dependent subjects during decision making predict relapse. *Archives of General Psychiatry*, 62, 761-768.

Pierce v. Society of Sisters, 268 U.S. 510 (1925).

Prince v. Massachusetts, 321 U.S. 158, 166 (1944).

Public Law No. 104-120; Section 110 Statute 834 (Mar. 28, 1996). 42 U.S.C. Section 1437d(1)(5) 1997.

Putnam, R.D. (2000). *Bowling alone: The collapse and revival of American community*. New York: Simon & Schuster.

Rawson, R.A. & Anglin, M.D. (1999). *Methamphetamine: New knowledge, new treatments.*

Regier, D.A., Farmer, M. E., Rae, D. S., Locke, B. Z., Keith, S. J., Judd, L. L., et al. (1990). Comorbidity of mental disorders with alcohol and other drug abuse—Results from the epidemiologic catchment area (ECA) study. *Journal of the American Medical Association*, 264, 2511–2518.

Rempel, M., Fox-Kralstein, D., Cissner, A., Cohen, R., Labriola, M., & Farole, D., et al. (2003). *The New York State adult drug court evaluation: Policies, participants and impacts.* New York, NY: Center for Court Innovation.

Report to Congress on the prevention and treatment of co-occurring substance abuse disorders and mental disorders. (2002). Substance Abuse and Mental Health Services Administration, U.S. Department of Health and Human Services, Washington D.C.

Report to the legislature: efforts to contain per capita cost of adoption support and foster care services, Chapter 518, Laws of 2005, Section 202(6). (2006). Department of Social & Health Services Children's Administration, Finance and Operations Support Division, Olympia, WA.

Roman, J., Townsend, W., & Bhati, A. (2003). *Recidivism rates for drug court graduates: Nationally based estimates.* Urban Institute and Caliber Associates, New York.

Rosack, J. (2004). Treatment of meth users should target mood-disorder symptoms. *Psychiatric News*, 39, 73-84.

Rossman, S.B., Roman, J., Zweig, J.M., Rempel, M., & Lindquist, C. (2011). *The Multi-site Adult Drug Court Evaluation: Executive Summary* (Pre-Production). Urban Institute.

Ryan, J.P., Marsh J.C.,Testa M.F., & Louderman R. (2006). Integrating substance abuse treatment and child welfare services: Findings from Illinois alcohol and other drug abuse waiver demonstration. *Social Work Research*, 30, 95-108.

Sampson, R.J, & Laub, J.H. (1993). *Crime in the making: Pathways and turning points through life*. Cambridge, MA: Harvard University Press.

Sampson, R.J. and Laub, J.H. (2003). *Shared beginnings, divergent lives: Delinquent boys to age 70.* Cambridge, MA: Harvard University Press.

Sampson, R.J. and Laub, J.H. (2005). A life-course view of the development of crime. *Annals of the American Academy of Political and Social Science*, 602, 12-45.

Satel, S.L. (1999). *Drug treatment: The case for coercion.* Washington D.C.: American Enterprise Institute, Studies in Social Welfare Policy Series.

Schroeder, R.D., Giordano, P.C. & Cernkovich, S.A. (2007). Drug use and desistance processes. *Criminology*, 45, 191-222.

Sentencing Reform Act of 1984. (1984). Pub. L. No. 98-473, § 211, 98 Stat. 1987.

Shah, R. (2002). *Public health concerns from the epidemic of methamphetamine abuse.* Presentation to the Minnesota Department of Health, Minneapolis, MN.

Shah, M.F., Mancuso, D., He, L., Estee, S., Felver, B., Beall, K., and Fiedler, F. (December 2010). Behavioral Health Risk among TANF Parents: Links to Homelessness, Child Abuse and Arrests. *Report to the Division of Behavioral Health and Recovery,* Washington State DSHS Research and Data Analysis Division.

Simons, R. L., Stewart, E., Gordon, L. C., Conger, R. D., & Elder, G. H. (2002). A test of life-course explanations for stability and change in antisocial behavior from adolescence to young adulthood. *Criminology, 40*, 401-434.

Simpson, D. D., & Flynn, P. M. (2008). Drug Abuse Treatment Outcome Studies (DATOS): A national evaluation of treatment effectiveness. In G. Fisher & N. Roget (Eds.), *Encyclopedia of Substance Abuse Prevention, Treatment, and Recovery* (pp. 303-307). Thousand Oaks, CA: Sage Publishing.

Simpson, D.D., Joe, G. W., & Brown, B.S. (1997). Treatment retention and follow-up outcomes in the Drug Abuse Treatment Outcome Study (DATOS). *Psychology of Addictive Behaviors*, 11:4, 294-307.

Simpson, D.D., & Sells, S.B. (1982). Effectiveness of treatment for drug abuse: An overview of the DARP research program. *Advances in Alcohol and Substance Abuse,* 2, 7-29.

Stanley v. Illinois, 405 U.S. 645 (1972).

Stark, M.J. (1992). Dropping out of substance abuse treatment: a clinically oriented review. *Clinical Psychology Review*, 12, 93-116.

Substance Abuse and Mental Health Services Administration, Office of Applied Studies. *Treatment Episode Data Set (TEDS): 1996-2006. National Admissions to Substance Abuse Treatment Services*, DASIS Series: S-43, DHHS Publication No. (SMA) 08-4347, Rockville, MD, 2008.

Substance Abuse and Mental Health Services Administration, *Results from the 2010 National Survey on Drug Use and Health: Summary of National Findings*, NSDUH Series H-41, HHS Publication No. (SMA) 11-4658. Rockville, MD: Substance Abuse and Mental Health Services Administration, 2011.

Tauber, J. (1999). National Institute of Drug Abuse (NIDA) Fact Sheet.

Terry, III, C,W. (1999). Judicial change and dedicated treatment courts: Case studies in innovation. In C.W Terry, III (ed.), *The Early Drug Courts: Case Studies in Judicial Innovation.* (pp. 1, 7-8). Thousand Oaks, California: Sage Publications.

Thomas, W., & Znaniecki, F. (1920). *The Polish Peasant in Europe and America.* R.G. Badger, Boston.

Thornberry , T.P., & Krohn, M.D. (2003). *Taking stock of delinquency: An overview of findings from contemporary longitudinal studies.* New York: Kluwer Academic/Plenum Publishers.

Toufexis, A. (1991). Innocent victims. *Time*, 137, 56-62.

Trujillo, B. (2004). Self-organizing legal systems: Precedent and variation in bankruptcy. *Utah Law Review*, 483, 528-543.

Turley, M., & Sibley, A. (2001). *Dallas County DIVERT court outcome evaluation.* Report to the Dallas County DIVERT Court, Dallas, TX.

U.S. Census Bureau, Profile of Selected Housing Characteristics: 2000.

U.S. Department of Health and Human Services, Administration for Children and Families, Administration on Children, Youth and Families, Children's Bureau, (2011). *The AFCARS (Adoption and Foster Care Analysis and Reporting System) report preliminary FY 2010 estimates as of June 2011 (18).*

U.S. Department of Health and Human Services, Substance Abuse and Mental Health Services Administration. (2009). *SAMHSA Portfolio of Programs and Activities.*

U.S. Department of Health and Human Services, Substance Abuse and Mental Health Services Administration. (2006a). *ATR (Access to Recovery) State Targets.*

U.S. Department of Health and Human Services, Substance Abuse and Mental Health Services Administration. (2006b). *SAMHSA Access to Recovery (ATR) grants summary of state target areas and target populations.*

U.S. Department of Health and Human Services, Centers for Disease Control and Prevention, National Center for Health Statistics. (2005). Death rates for suicide, according to sex, race, Hispanic origin, and age: United States, selected years 1950–2003. In Health, United States, 2005 with chartbook on trends in the health of Americans, Table 46, p. 221.

U.S. Department of Health and Human Services, Substance Abuse and Mental Health Services Administration, Office of Applied Studies. (2009). *National survey of substance abuse treatment services (N-SSATS) 2009 data on substance abuse treatment facilities.*

U.S. Department of Health and Human Services, Substance Abuse and Mental Health Services Administration, Office of Applied Studies. (2009). *National survey of substance abuse, treatment services (N-SSATS) 2009 data on substance abuse treatment facilities in Washington State.*

U.S. Department of Housing and Urban Development v. Pearlie Rucker, et al. Nos. 00-1770 and 00-1781. March 26, 2002.

U.S. Department of Justice, Office of Justice Programs, Bureau of Justice Assistance Bulletin. (May 2005). *Drug courts: An effective strategy for communities facing methamphetamine.*

Volkow, N.D. (2004). The Reality of Comorbidity: Depression and Drug Abuse. *Biological Psychiatry*, 56, 714-717.

Washington Administrative Code (WAC) 388-15-009. (2003). *What is child abuse or neglect?*

Washington State Constitution Article I, Section 7- *Invasion of Private Affairs or Home Prohibited.*

Washington State Department of Labor and Industries. (2005). *History of Washington Minimum Wage.*

Watkins, K.E., Hunter, S.B., Burnam, M.A., Pincus, H.A., & Nicholson, G. (2005). Review of treatment recommendations for persons with a co-occurring affective or anxiety and substance use disorder. *Psychiatric Services*, 56, 913-926.

Weintraub, S. (1990-91). Children and adolescents at risk for substance abuse and psychopathology. *International Journal of Addiction*, 25, 481-494.

Weisdorf, T., Parran, T.V., Graham, A., & Snyder, C. (1999). Comparison of pregnancy-specific interventions to a traditional treatment program for cocaine- addicted pregnant women. *Journal of Substance Abuse Treatment*, 16, 43-44.

Wexler, D., & Winick, B. (1996). *Law in a therapeutic key: Developments in therapeutic jurisprudence.* Durham, NC: Carolina Academic Press.

White, W. (1998). *Slaying the dragon: The history of addiction treatment and recovery in America.* Bloomington, IL: Chestnut Health Systems.

Wilens, T., & Biederman, J. (1993). Psychopathology in preadolescent children at high risk for substance abuse. A review of the literature. *Harvard Review of Psychiatry*, 1, 207-218.

Wolock, I., & Magura, S. (1996). Parental substance abuse as a predictor of child maltreatment reports. *Child Abuse & Neglect*, 20, 1183-1193.

Worcel, S., Furrer, C., Green, B.L. & Rhodes, B. (2006). *Family treatment drug court evaluation final Phase I study report.* Portland, OR: NPC Research.

Worcel, S. D., Furrer, C. J., Green, B. L., Burrus, S. W. M., & Finigan, M. W. (Nov. 2008). Effects of family treatment drug courts on substance abuse and child welfare outcomes. *Child Abuse Review, 17*(6), 427-443.

Young, N. K., (2005). *Fighting meth in America's heartland: Assessing the impact on local law enforcement and child welfare agencies.* Statement before the U.S. House of Representatives Government Reform Subcommittee on Criminal Justice, Drug Policy, and Human Resources.

Index